HAPPY DOG

ADAMS MEDIA

NEW YORK   LONDON   TORONTO   SYDNEY   NEW DELHI

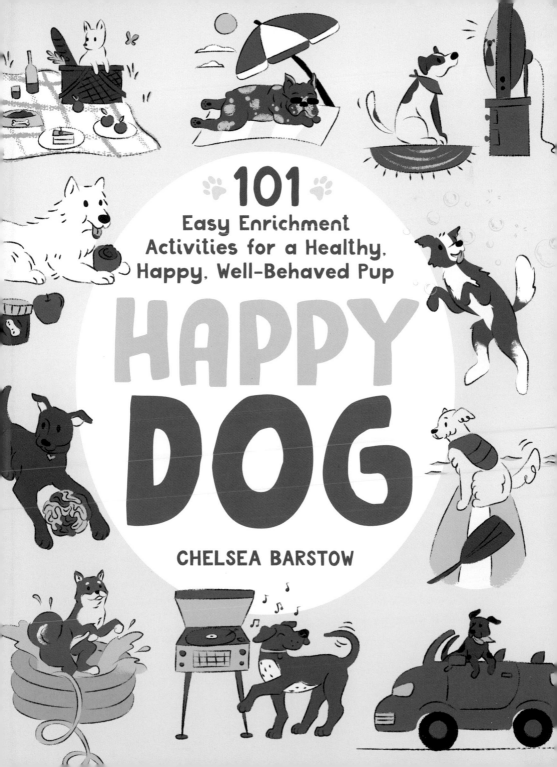

101
Easy Enrichment Activities for a Healthy, Happy, Well-Behaved Pup

HAPPY
DOG

CHELSEA BARSTOW

Adamsmedia

Adams Media
An Imprint of Simon & Schuster, Inc.
100 Technology Center Drive
Stoughton, Massachusetts 02072

First Adams Media hardcover edition
December 2023

ADAMS MEDIA and colophon are
registered trademarks of Simon &
Schuster, Inc.

For information about special
discounts for bulk purchases, please
contact Simon & Schuster Special
Sales at 1-866-506-1949 or
business@simonandschuster.com.

The Simon & Schuster Speakers
Bureau can bring authors to your
live event. For more information or
to book an event, contact the Simon
& Schuster Speakers Bureau at
1-866-248-3049 or visit our website
at www.simonspeakers.com.

Interior design by Erin Alexander
Illustrations by Tess Armstrong

Manufactured in China

10 9 8 7 6 5 4 3 2 1

Library of Congress Cataloging-in-
Publication Data
Names: Barstow, Chelsea, author.
Title: Happy dog / Chelsea Barstow.
Other titles: 101 easy enrichment
activities for a healthy, happy,
well-behaved pup
Description: First Adams Media
hardcover edition. | Stoughton,
Massachusetts: Adams Media, 2023. |
Includes bibliographical references
and index.
Identifiers: LCCN 2023024295 |
ISBN 9781507221075 (hc) |
ISBN 9781507221082 (ebook)
Subjects: LCSH: Dogs--Behavior. |
Dogs--Behavior therapy.
Classification: LCC SF433 .B3448
2023 | DDC 636.7/0887--dc23/
eng/20230530
LC record available at
https://lccn.loc.gov/2023024295

ISBN 978-1-5072-2107-5
ISBN 978-1-5072-2108-2 (ebook)

The information in this book is provided
to engage, educate, and enhance the
reader's knowledge and understanding
of dogs. It is not meant to be a
substitute for professional veterinary
care. If your dog is showing any signs of
distress or if you suspect your dog is ill,
contact your veterinarian immediately
for diagnosis and treatment of any
illness or injury. The author and
publisher disclaim any liability arising
directly or indirectly from the use of the
information in this book.

🐾 Dedication 🐾

To Tim, Levi, & Cricket

Acknowledgments

I cannot begin to express my thanks to my husband, Tim, who is always ready for the next adventure, offered his unparalleled support, and repeatedly said yes to my suggestions for adding each dog to our family. I'm extremely grateful to my parents for always encouraging me to follow my heart throughout my career and life path, and my sister, Marissa, for her video chat sessions to offer her support and love from states away.

Special thanks to Chrissy and Chris, my first zookeeping mentors, who took a chance on me as an indecisive nineteen-year-old college student and introduced me to the incredible world of animal enrichment.

I also want to thank all at Adams Media who made this book possible, especially Eileen and Jennifer for your guidance and advice. Writing this book has been a dream come true and was made possible by you all.

Contents

Chapter 2: Food Enrichment / 61

Chapter 3: Sensory Enrichment / 93

Chapter 4: Cognitive Enrichment / 125

Chapter 5: Social Enrichment / 155

Chapter 6: Miscellaneous Enrichment / 185

Introduction

Your dog deserves only the best! The best food. The best toys. The best care. But while all good dog owners want to give their furry friend a fulfilling and long life, they often miss an essential part of a dog's mental exercise and capability: enrichment.

Canine enrichment is a way for your dog to embrace their natural urges (sniffing, digging, tugging) in a safe, healthy, and productive way. Enrichment exercises, when used properly, challenge your pup's brain, making them more well adjusted and content overall. In *Happy Dog*, you'll find everything you need to know about enrichment and how to begin your individual pooch's journey to a joyful, more fulfilled life. In the first part of the book, you'll learn that enrichment gives your dog a sense of control over their environment, which can reduce their stress and build your relationship. And these types of activities are easy to incorporate by creating a schedule for your pup's play and following safety guidelines.

After a comprehensive look at what enrichment is and how to modify things safely and comfortably for your individual dog, in Part 2, you get access to 101 fun and unique enrichment activities that challenge your dog in different ways. Some of the customizable activities include:

- Changing up your dog's space by creating a raised dirt bed.
- Challenging your pup's snack drive by having them solve the egg carton game.
- Playing with your pet's five senses by going on a scent stroll.
- Engaging your dog's problem-solving by playing the object permanence game.
- Shining a light on your dog's extroverted side by visiting with dog friends.

There's so much to explore and learn throughout these pages, so get your schedule out and drop in an activity a day for your favorite furry friend. Your dog will thank you in their own way—whether that's a kiss or a lap cuddle—and you get the satisfaction of a worn-out and truly *happy* dog!

PART 1

Introducing Enrichment

You love your dogs and want what's best for them. Whether your dog is a down-to-earth Doodle or an athletic Golden Retriever, you want them to have a great life. To do that, you need to be familiar with canine enrichment and the types of enrichment activities your dog likes the most.

Here, you'll learn all about enrichment and how you can tailor it to your own dog's needs with the six enrichment categories and the four Cs. We'll also go over how to give enrichment safely and responsibly, how to view the world from your dog's perspective, and how to recognize fear/stress behaviors. You'll also learn how to easily incorporate enrichment into your weekly schedule without feeling overwhelmed while discovering how to end every day with a happy dog. Before digging into those topics, you should first get a better understanding of what enrichment is!

What Is Enrichment?

It's amazing to think that dogs have only been domesticated for about thirty thousand years! Yet, to this day, domestic dogs and wolves share over 98 percent of their DNA. This means that modern dogs share some of the same natural behaviors as their wolf ancestors. These behaviors, many of which people sometimes see as undesirable or dangerous, include digging, chewing, jumping, and chasing. While it's not impossible, it can be hard work to completely train your dog not to chew up the couch or chase the cat.

It's incredible that people have learned to live with dogs, but of course, living with a creature that doesn't speak your language is hard. With this in mind, animal behaviorists have researched and found a way to better dogs' lives through enrichment activities. Enrichment allows dogs to display these oftentimes unwanted behaviors safely and responsibly. These activities will not only keep your dog occupied during the day, but will also create a happy, tired, and satisfied dog at night.

Enrichment is an activity that allows your dog to display a natural behavior in a way that is both acceptable to you (and your home) and safe for your pup. It gives your dog the freedom of choice and provides an outlet for them to relieve any stress that may build up during the day, which can come from something as simple as a visit to the veterinarian or seeing an unfamiliar dog walk by their window. Enrichment activities will allow your dog to explore and display their natural behaviors, such as sniffing for food or other scents, digging, and running, along with many other behaviors. Not all enrichment activities work your dog physically. Many exercises will be challenging to your dog's mind, which can be just as exhausting as a physical challenge. Some examples include teaching your dog a new behavior or testing out their sniffing skills.

The Six Enrichment Categories

When creating an enrichment plan for your dog, there are a number of different types of enrichment activities you need to consider. Here you'll find activities divided up into the following categories: environmental, food, sensory, cognitive, social, and miscellaneous. The miscellaneous category includes activities that may involve some, all, or none of the other categories but will still stimulate your dog. Taking activities from these six categories may help you achieve a successful enrichment plan for your own pup, which will be completely unique in comparison with another dog. One furry friend may enjoy social enrichment, while another may react well to sensory enrichment.

Some activities may overlap, but they are categorized by the most prominent way your dog is enriched. The chapters throughout this book will go into further detail about each category, but here is a general idea of each:

- **Environmental enrichment:** any activity that changes your dog's physical environment, whether within your home or outside of it. This can include activities such as Go on a Hike or Put Toys on Rotation.
- **Food enrichment:** an activity that presents your dog with food in any other way besides their typical food bowl. This can be something like the activities Use Slow Feeder Bowls or Try a Rapid-Fire Mealtime.
- **Sensory enrichment:** an activity that works one or more of your dog's five senses: sight, sound, smell, taste, or touch. Sensory enrichment can include activities such as Go on a Scent Stroll or Make a Frozen Pup-Sicle.
- **Cognitive enrichment:** an activity that works your dog mentally rather than physically. Cognitive enrichment includes

many games, such as Play Hide-and-Seek or Play the Object Permanence Game.

- **Social enrichment:** an activity that grants your dog access to an opportunity for companionship, whether with other dogs, people, or something else. Example activities are Find a Dog-Friendly Coffee Shop or Visit with Old Friends.
- **Miscellaneous enrichment:** an activity that doesn't quite fit into any of the other categories but still serves an essential purpose in enriching your dog's life. Miscellaneous enrichment includes activities such as Grow an Herb Garden or Use a Flirt Pole.

Each enrichment activity will stimulate a dog's natural behavior, which in turn will release excess energy and promote calming behaviors. Some of these activities don't take long to set up at all and can keep your pooch tired out for hours!

The Four Cs of Enrichment

Ensure your pup has the tools to succeed in any enrichment activity with the four Cs of enrichment! The four Cs of enrichment are guidelines that consider standards of care before and during an enrichment activity and provide advice about how to approach your dog's behaviors. These guidelines have been used in zoos, sanctuaries, and farms for all different kinds of animals. For canine enrichment, the four Cs include comfort, challenge, choice, and change. These four requirements must be met in order to provide proper enrichment to your dog.

- **Comfort:** You must meet your dog's basic needs first, which include proper food and water access, shelter, and freedom from chronic stress. Chronic stress is caused by lack of security, which dogs can experience from not knowing if and when they will be fed or being uncomfortable in their home. A dog suffers from being around people or other animals that mistreat them and not being able to remove themselves from the situation.

- **Challenge:** When you begin an enrichment activity with your dog, you must keep in mind that it may not work for your dog right away. Each exercise may need tailoring to fit your dog's needs because the exercises as written may not appropriately align with *your* dog's intelligence or capabilities. An exercise that is too easy may get boring, but an exercise that is too difficult can cause frustration, leading to inappropriate destructive behaviors, such as ripping up an item that was not meant to be destroyed. The appropriate balance is somewhere in the middle.
- **Choice:** Your dog should always have the freedom of choice during any enrichment activity—don't force something that they aren't interested in! They are free to walk away and not participate at any point. You can do this by giving your dog access to their crate or keeping the door to another room open so your dog can easily leave.
- **Change:** Variety is the key! Enrichment should be a deviation from your everyday routine, although it does not have to be complicated. Something as small as switching your dog's food bowl to another type of bowl counts as enrichment.

When your dog's training and care involve the four Cs, you will see your dog's unique personality begin to appear during their enrichment activities. This is because you are offering them a comfortable place to learn, providing more advanced (or less advanced) steps so they can fully engage their brains, and switching things up to keep them preoccupied.

Individualizing Enrichment

Just like humans, each dog is different and has their own individual needs. So, your dog probably won't absolutely love every activity— no matter how much you may want to have your dog run through a homemade snow maze or take them to eat their dinner in the park. As their caretaker, you should always be sure to enrich the dog who's in front of you. These needs may change based on their personality, past experiences, age, breed, and other factors you have no control over. As your dog experiences changes in life, such as adding another dog to the family or developing arthritis with age, they may prefer different types of enrichment. And that's okay!

When looking at breed needs, you may find that high-drive breeds, such as Border Collies or German Shepherds, enjoy higher-energy activities requiring more physical or cognitive aspects. In contrast, lower-drive breeds, such as Saint Bernards or French Bulldogs, may enjoy passive enrichment activities. Your dog's breed is a great place to start determining what they might like, but do not be surprised if your dog's favorite activities contrast with their breed. What works for one Old English Sheepdog may not work for yours.

If you have a dog with unknown or mixed breeds, you can just as quickly figure out which activities they may enjoy by observing their day-to-day behaviors. Perhaps you've recently brought your dog into your home; it may take a few months to get to know and understand your dog's personality and quirks. Still, you will notice your dog's preferences eventually, and they may turn out to be different than your expectations. For example, one of my dogs, Levi, is an American Pit Bull Terrier (APBT) mixed with Australian Cattle Dog (ACD) and Mastiff. ACD mixes typically like herding activities, as they are herding dogs, but though that's in his DNA, he has no ability or drive to herd. That's why I tailor his enrichment plan to include more chasing activities, which engage his higher prey drive.

It's my job as his owner to find which enrichment will be best for his personality. The same goes for you and your dog—you only get to know what they like by spending time with them and monitoring how they react to each activity.

Throughout trying the many activities in this book, you may find your dog enjoys surprising types of enrichment. As their guardian, it's up to you to know your dog and their needs, but don't be afraid to try a new activity that challenges them. Just be sure to look out for fear and frustration behaviors, which this book will touch on in the Enrichment Safety and Responsibility section. As you try new activities, feel free to mark the pages with notes (and utilize the note pages in each chapter) about your dog's reaction to remember which ones to go back to and which ones your dog would turn their nose up at. The designated notes pages are also a great space to write down any alterations to an activity that really helped your pup focus and get their energy out.

Enrichment Safety and Responsibility

While enrichment is supposed to be fun and work your dog's brain, it is not a babysitter. In most cases, you should supervise your dog when doing enrichment activities. You may need to take a different approach if you have a dog with separation anxiety: Ask a dog behaviorist to advise you if enrichment would benefit your dog when you're not around. However, for dogs without separation anxiety, supervision is required! As their owner, you must practice each enrichment activity you set out to do with your dog's unique quirks in mind: whether that means providing them with booties for the cold or clearing inedible material after a toy is ripped during enrichment.

Pica

Pica, a condition where dogs eat items that are not supposed to be consumed and have no nutritional value, is a serious condition. Pica can include the consumption of dog toy stuffing, nonedible items from the trash, fabric, or many other household items and is not the same as your dog going through a puppy phase. Puppies tend to grow out of the phase of putting everything in their mouths; however, pica can develop in adult or senior dogs and can be diagnosed by your vet. This book has many activities that are appropriate for dogs with pica or dogs still in their chewing puppy phase.

Household Item Destruction

Keep in mind, destruction is different from consuming inedible items. An appropriate response to some enrichment activities will be for your dog to destroy the item, but you must ensure they don't eat nonfood materials. Many people ask whether destruction-themed enrichment encourages other destruction in your home, such as your dog going through the garbage or nibbling the legs of your couch. In short, your dog may perform these destructive behaviors no matter what. Enrichment, however, gives them the proper and safe outlet to perform these behaviors and will decrease the probability that your dog will choose an inappropriate time, place, or item. It's also important to remember that dogs take many social cues from you as their owner and look to you for guidance. If your dog sees that you are the happiest when they destroy a toy and you are unhappy when they ruin your shoe, they are more likely to continue to play with the toy over the shoe in the future.

Using Food Properly in Enrichment

Enrichment is not a replacement for a proper diet or exercise plan but instead should work in harmony with them. Your dog's health is super important! Give them proper meals as recommended by your veterinarian. However, if you use treats during enrichment, most veterinarians recommend that the caloric value of treats should not exceed 10 percent of your dog's daily caloric needs. The calories and other nutritional information of treats should always be listed on the back of the bag or box. Training treats are typically smaller and therefore have fewer calories, making them a great choice for food enrichment activities.

Some alternative options for using extra food in enrichment include using your dog's regular meal during their activity or using a low-calorie food item, such as romaine lettuce or deveined celery pieces. You can also use plain Greek yogurt, bananas, and blueberries (whole or mashed). If you have a baby in the house, or would rather use something shelf-stable, you can actually use dog-friendly puréed baby food. To determine if it's dog friendly, always look at the label to ensure every ingredient is dog safe. The best puréed baby food to get has the simplest ingredients, such as plain sweet potato or plain pumpkin. If you're unsure about a particular ingredient, contact your veterinarian.

Fear and Frustration in Enrichment Activities

As discussed earlier, each dog's enrichment must be individualized. Some activities may cause fear in one dog, while the activity may be super fun for another. Any enrichment exercise should not induce fear in your dog. If you see any signs of fear, stop the activity immediately. Dogs show signs of stress through their body language, and it can be very subtle, such as a small tongue flick. Other signs to look out for include rigid body language, pinned

ears, tucked tail, trying to hide, or shaking. If you're unsure of dog stress signals, ask a dog trainer or look up videos on *YouTube*.

Other activities may be too challenging for dogs. Throughout the chapters, you are given the most straightforward version of an enrichment activity and ways to increase the challenge if your dog is the star of the class. If your dog shows signs of frustration, either help them complete the exercise or take away an obvious obstacle. Signs of frustration to look out for include barking, jumping, losing interest in the activity, or redirected aggression.

How to See the World from a Dog's Eyes

When considering what enrichment to give your dog, try your best not to anthropomorphize them. Anthropomorphizing is an innate human behavior where people attribute their feelings to something else, in this instance, dogs. It's normal for you to put yourself in your pooch's shoes and believe what you feel would be what they feel. For example, most humans enjoy being hugged because it releases the happy chemicals in their brains and is a natural primate behavior, so it is common for people to embrace dogs. However, hugging is not an instinctive canine behavior; a pup may show signs of stress during a hug. Therefore, it's vital to consider a dog's natural behaviors and how you can let your dog be a dog.

Contrafreeloading

Contrafreeloading is a perfect example of a dog's natural behavior that is very different from humans. Contrafreeloading is a behavior observed in nature where some species of animal prefer to work for their food versus getting it without any effort or for free. You can experiment with your own dog to observe contrafreeloading for yourself. Split your dog's meal into their regular food bowl and a food puzzle that they have to solve to get the food. Which do they go after first? Most likely, they will head to solve the puzzle first, especially if the puzzle is in a blue- or yellow-colored bowl.

Dog Vision

Another way to view the world from your dog's perspective is by thinking about how they literally see the world. While not fully col-orblind, dogs see fewer colors than humans do because they have dichromatic (two cones) vision, while humans have trichromatic (three cones) vision. A dog's sense of sight is not their primary sense since dogs most often use their sense of smell to take in most of the world around them. Most humans can see and decipher every color in the rainbow. Dogs can see blue, yellow, and gray. These colors are important to remember when making an enrichment plan for your dog. Blue and yellow are colors that will pop to them, such as tennis balls, and although you don't have to stick to that color palette in your dog's enrichment, adding blue or yellow toys into their plan every now and again may be more enticing.

When you begin to view the world from your dog's perspective, it is easier to come up with and develop an enrichment plan. You will learn what they like and may not like. When you get to know your dog better, it can also help you develop a solid foundation in your relationship and build trust.

How to Create an Enrichment Plan

In an ideal world, your dog(s) would get different enrichment daily. However, that may not be realistic for you! Between work, educa-tion, taking care of kids, hobbies, and trying to enjoy your social

lives, there's only so much time in the day. It's easier to start slowly by introducing your dog to enrichment, and as you get more in tune with what activities enrich your dog, you will be able to create them more quickly and more often.

Basics of Enrichment Planning

Enrichment should not take up hours of a day. Your dog does not need to be entertained endlessly. It's actually more detrimental if they are constantly stimulated because they can build up a tolerance that can never be quenched, resulting in dogs who can never settle. Learning to rest is just as important as having time put aside for enrichment. Do not feel guilty if you only have twenty minutes a day to do this incredible exercise for your dog's well-being. Beginning small is better than never trying at all.

You may also pick up on when your dog has days when they need more enrichment than other times. They may communicate this through restlessness, attention-seeking behaviors, or boredom/destructive behaviors. On these days, it is helpful to have a backup enrichment activity planned, such as a frozen lick mat or an extra walk. Like us, dogs have some days when they want to be lazy and others when they are energized and ready for adventure.

Scheduling Enrichment Training Sessions

If you like to keep lists or calendars, this is a great time to use those skills. Create a weekly calendar and try to incorporate each enrichment category on a rotation schedule. For example, try food enrichment on Monday, social enrichment on Wednesday, and cognitive enrichment on Friday. Then the next week, try environmental enrichment on Monday, sensory enrichment on Wednesday, and a miscellaneous enrichment activity on Friday. Then begin the following week again with food enrichment. Rotating a schedule keeps your enrichment activities fresh and fun and challenges your dog physically and mentally (and decreases your own mental load). You can start with activities in this book that you know your dog will like and continue to add in new activities to challenge your dog. This book has plenty of ideas to help you think of new activities in all six enrichment categories, and you may decide to build off of them to create something completely unique for your dog. There are also many ways that you can increase the challenge of repeat enrichment activities, many of which are explained throughout the 101 enrichment activities.

Now that you have learned about why enrichment is so necessary for every dog and that dogs may react differently to different forms of enrichment, it's time to get into the exciting 101 enrichment activities this book has in store. These carefully constructed activities are fun for your dog, easy to set up, and can be easily modified as needed. At the end of the day, you'll have a relaxed and happy dog. Have fun!

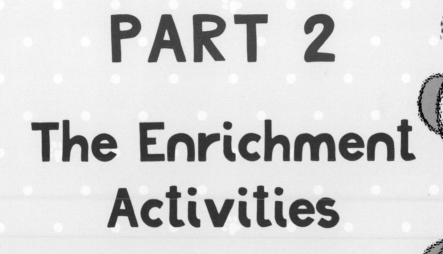

PART 2

The Enrichment Activities

CHAPTER 1

Environmental Enrichment

Your dog is not loving the new season of your guilty pleasure show as much as you are! Time to get outside (or change up the decor on the inside) for a fun and simple set of activities all categorized as environmental enrichment. This enrichment type involves switching up your pup's day-to-day physical space. You and your pup could visit totally new places, or, if it's a rainy day, you could alter their surroundings in the comfort of your home. Most of these activities don't even require you to purchase anything new. That said, the activities may depend on the climate, as well as the location, of where you live.

Walk and Smell the Flowers

Spring and early summer is a time full of new growth and beauty outdoors! When the weather starts warming up and flowers begin to pop up, it's the perfect time to take your dog on a flower-smelling walk. Some dog-friendly flowers you can look out for include roses (but be wary of the thorny branches that can get stuck in their fur), snapdragons, marigolds, sunflowers, and zinnias.

How to Do It

1. Take your dog for a walk around your neighborhood to find dog-friendly flowers.
2. Allow your dog to smell the flowers and investigate them.
3. The flowers listed above are all safe to ingest in small amounts, so it's okay if your dog takes a bite or two. (If the flowers are in a neighbor's yard, make sure to get that person's approval before your dog takes a bite.)

> ### Safety Tip
> Be on the lookout to see if your neighbors are using pesticides on their flowers (there will usually be a sign in their yard), and have your dog avoid those flowers.

How It Helps

Spring flowers only sprout once a year. Because of their seasonality, they can help to switch up your dog's environment as well as their walking routine.

Go to the Beach

Nowadays, there are so many dog-friendly beaches and lakes you can take your dog to. Whether you live near one or plan on traveling, bringing your dog can help to switch up their everyday routine and environment and give them a chance to explore something new. If you plan on doing this activity, be sure to watch that your dog does not consume anything in your chosen location. Drinking ocean or lake water can be dangerous for your dog.

How to Do It

1. Pack a leash or long lead (a really long leash), water with a water bowl, and treats if needed to help encourage exploration from your dog or reward their recall behavior.
2. Decide where you want to bring your dog. Make sure that the location is dog friendly and double-check your town's leash laws. If leashes are required, using a long lead will work best. If leashes are not required and your dog has a strong recall behavior, utilize the opportunity to give your dog off-leash time.
3. Make sure to always supervise your dog wherever you bring them, especially if they will be around water. As a precaution, a long leash may come in handy. This is also the time where you can break out your dog's life vest if they want to go swimming. Make sure it is on properly (zipped up all the way or buckled securely around them) before your dog gets into the water.
4. Encourage exploration, without consumption, of the sand and the water. You can encourage this by participating in the activity yourself. Dip your toes into the water, and your dog may follow suit.

How It Helps

Sometimes, your dog can get stuck in a mundane routine—just like humans do. The fresh air, the sand between their paw pads, watching other animals (such as seagulls), and maybe even a swim in the water may be just what your dog needs to get out some extra energy. Yes, it might be a big ordeal to get your dog to the beach, but it's well worth it!

Put Toys on Rotation

Keeping a rotation of your dog's favorite toys, instead of making any or all toys available at a time, will not only create novelty but will also be a money saver. It is also an easy and free way to incorporate enrichment into your dog's life. The toys will be familiar but will have a sense of newness to them, making the lives of the toys last a bit longer! Your pup's toys will also likely last longer when you monitor their playtime—not allowing them to chew up their newest plush in a matter of days.

How to Do It

1. Divide up your dog's toys into two or three groups. You can keep one or two of each kind of toy. For example, keep a plush toy, a ball, and a tug toy in each group.
2. Give one group of toys to your dog and put the others away in a safe place where your dog can't reach or get to them.
3. After two to three weeks, rotate the group of toys and switch the current group out for another group of toys. Wash the rotated-out toys as needed to keep them sanitary. You should also inspect each toy as you rotate them to check that they are still safe for playing.

🐾 Pet Pointers 🐾

Is it time to throw a toy away? A toy has reached the end of its life span when it becomes a hazard to your dog. This can include threads coming loose or undone, holes big enough for squeakers to come out and become a choking hazard, or small pieces breaking off the toy.

How It Helps

Oftentimes, dogs can become blind to toys and enrichment materials if they are easily accessible all the time. Your pup will become bored of familiar items. This boredom may create strain on pet parents, so they feel like they need to constantly provide new toys when that isn't the case. Although it may be tempting to buy the latest toy you saw on social media, it's not always necessary. Switching out groups of toys as dogs become bored of them creates novelty and excitement over their "new" toys. This is also a great opportunity for you to see which toys your dog may favor over others. Your pooch may prefer squeaky toys over chewing toys, which can help you when purchasing new toys in the future—after the old toys have truly reached the end of their life span. Your dog will have favorites; it may just take a rotation group or two to find it.

Go for a Stress-Free Stroll

As long as it's not freezing, raining, or way too hot, stress-free strolls are a free and easy way to switch up your dog's daily walk. This is the kind of walk where you give your dog the choice of where to go and let them take their time in a familiar setting.

How to Do It

1. Gather all the items you need for a regular walk. If it's a hot day, pack a light backpack with some water for you and your pup.
2. While on your stress-free stroll, allow your dog to pick the path (within reason).
3. Let them sniff and decide which way to go—just make sure you know how to get back!

How It Helps

This activity helps to de-stress your dog. You are allowing them the freedom of choice and to display their natural behaviors, such as sniffing. Your stress-free stroll may be just as tiring for your dog as a regular walk!

Switch Up Your Walking Routine

Just like humans, your pooch may find it easy (and boring) to go through the same routines every day. There are many instances where routines work well for your dog, but that doesn't mean you can't switch it up within your routine! Shifting something as minute as where you walk can make a huge difference to your dog, keeping them alert.

How to Do It

1. Pick a different route to walk each day or a few times a week. By varying the setting, your dog will be more interested in what's going on around them.
2. If you don't have many options for different routes, go on your normal walking route in reverse.

How It Helps

Walking a different route than normal works your dog's brain more than you think. Every walk you take is a chance for your dog to take in their environment. That means that every time you take a slightly different route, it's a brand-new opportunity for them to process and enjoy the novelty.

Create a Raised Dirt Bed

Now, with this activity, you may be thinking, "Why in the world would I purposefully give my dog dirt to dig in? Wouldn't that just encourage their digging behavior?" But remember the definition of enrichment! Enrichment is allowing your dog to display their natural behaviors in a safe manner. Your dog doesn't care if they are digging in your precious vegetable garden that you worked on all summer or if they get their own dirt patch to dig in. They just want to dig. This activity allows them to do it safely and will likely deter them from digging up those heirloom tomato vines. Unfortunately, this activity does require you to have a bit of your own outside space for the activity—or for you to be able to borrow a friend or family member's space on a regular basis.

How to Do It

1. Find an area in your yard that you can dedicate to building a raised dirt bed. This does not have to be an actual raised bed if you don't have the tools for one, but you want to create something that is differentiable from any other garden beds you have in your backyard. For something simple yet effective, use a kiddie pool. This will contain the mess and is still big enough for your dog to dig down into.
2. Fill your raised bed with dirt.
3. To get your dog to use the bed, give praise and treats when showing them the raised bed. Lure them onto the bed and watch their behavior. You can dig gently in the dirt with your hands to show them it's an acceptable place to let loose.

Safety Tip

If you want to avoid dirty, messy paws, you can also fill your bed with other dog-friendly substrates, such as cedar mulch. Avoid substrates that can become impacted if they are accidentally ingested, such as sand or pea gravel.

How It Helps

Digging is a natural dog behavior that many people see as destructive, and if dogs are not given the proper outlet, it can cause a lot of unwanted damage. Dogs take many cues from their owners, so if they see that you are happy and praise them when they dig in their designated spot versus when they dig in your vegetable garden, your dog will most likely go for their own spot the next time they get the urge to dig.

Build a Fort

This activity requires creativity and a space large enough to build a fort that is appropriately sized for your dog. If you have a small breed, such as a Dachshund, you can make a much smaller fort, while if you have a large breed, such as a Rottweiler, you will need to make it much bigger. You will want enough space for your dog to get in, get out, and turn around in it. Use blankets, pillows, couch cushions, or pretty much anything comfortable to build the fort of your dreams.

How to Do It

1. Gather all of your supplies and pick a spot in your home that is easily accessible to your dog. This can be somewhere your dog is comfortable, such as your bedroom or living room.
2. Build your fort in whatever way you choose while considering what your dog enjoys. For example, if they love to be under blankets, add in some extra blankets on the ground, or if they enjoy being in dark, enclosed areas, such as their crate, build something similar with your couch cushions. This is the time to use your imagination!
3. Avoid creating dangerous situations, such making a top-heavy fort or balancing blankets over lightweight chairs. Stay safe and create as sturdy of a fort as you can.
4. Enjoy the space with your dog or let your dog enjoy your work by themselves. Remember, this activity is primarily a space for them, so if you think they will have more fun exploring by themselves, let them be alone. However, make sure you are monitoring them so they do not engage in

unwanted behaviors, such as chewing on any furniture. You can also give them a long-lasting treat, such as a bully stick, to enjoy in the space.

> ## 🐾 Switch It Up 🐾
>
> If your dog is having a difficult time figuring out the activity, you can lure them with treats to check out the fort you made. You can also hide some of your dog's favorite toys within the fort as a fun surprise.

How It Helps

Many dogs enjoy the comfort of being in an enclosed space that is their own. By building them their own fort, they get the enjoyment of being in a space made just for them while switching up their routine of always being in their crate or a familiar room. They also have the choice of being in it or not, which can reduce stress and encourage relaxation behaviors. It can also be a great bonding activity if you and your dog decide to share the space together.

Go for a Swim

Swimming is greatly beneficial to your dog. Just like with humans, this low-impact workout is a wonderful way to get your dog moving, regardless of their age. It can help them to maintain a healthy body condition while being easy on their joints and muscles, making it an exceptional physical activity for older dogs who can't run around like they used to. It also gives you an opportunity to switch up your pup's daily environment!

How to Do It

1. Pick where you want to have your dog swim. Depending on the local laws and what bodies of water are available to you, this could be a beach, a lake, or a pool. Based on space in your backyard, you may opt for a family-sized blow-up pool—but watch your dog's nails!

2. Go slow when introducing your dog to swimming. Contrary to popular belief, dogs are not born with the knowledge of how to swim, so they must be taught. Start off with just getting their paws into the water so they can get used to the sensation of water. This may take some encouragement, which you can do by throwing a favorite toy into some shallow water or luring them to dip their paws in with a treat.

3. Use a properly fitting life jacket while your dog swims, and make sure their entire swim time is supervised. Most life jackets have a handle on them so you can help your dog to swim as they learn.

4. Start with quick swim sessions and work your way up to longer ones if your dog continues to enjoy the activity. If you decide to take your dog swimming in different bodies of water, you may have to start all over again with just getting your dog's toes wet, or they may love it from the start and jump right in!

> ### 🐾 Safety Tip 🐾
> Get your dog used to water before introducing them to swimming by giving baths, playing with the hose, or showing them the sprinkler in your backyard. A small inflatable pool for children where your dog is still able to stand may also be a great way to start out.

How It Helps

The seasonality of this exercise makes the enrichment different. Depending on where you live, swimming can typically only be done during warmer months. Just like with humans, water that is too cold can cause harm to your dog through hypothermia. Some dogs will be more at risk than others, including puppies or senior dogs as well as smaller breed dogs, like Chihuahuas. If your dog enjoys swimming and being around water, jumping in for the first time after a few winter months will be just as exciting as a new toy.

Navigate a Snow Maze

One of the best parts about dog enrichment is that you can use what you have around you, even if that means using the nature outside your front door. In the winter, you will have different (and exciting) enrichment opportunities due to the snow! If you get enough snow to shovel, take the opportunity to make a maze for your dog. All you will need for this activity is enough snow, a shovel, and a toy or treat. If your dog needs it, you can also use a dog snow jacket and boots to cover their paws.

How to Do It

1. Wait for a big snowstorm, and watch the snow pile up so there is enough to shovel into maze walls. Make sure the snow is appropriate for maze construction—powdery snow will not stay in the neat piles that are required for this activity. The snow should be packed a little and create small walls as you shovel a path.

2. Shovel or plow a maze for your dog to figure out. Try to make the walls tall enough to discourage cheating/jumping over the walls.

3. Hide a toy or treat at the end of the maze as a prize for your dog. You may have to lure or encourage them to figure out the maze, especially if it is their first time doing the activity.

4. Make sure your dog is properly outfitted for the weather if they need to be. Have them wear a coat or booties if they need them. Be sure to keep a close eye on your dog to make sure they are enjoying themselves and are not frustrated by the activity or too cold.

How It Helps

This is an activity that is seasonal, fun, and free. You can do a different maze each day if it snows multiple days in a row. This not only switches up their routine and environment, but it also challenges their mind because they are searching for the toy or treat at the end of the maze. It also challenges their senses since the snow on their paws will be cooler than the usual ground they walk on.

Desensitize Floor Materials

You may not think about the different things lying around your house on a day-to-day basis, but it's important (especially for puppies) to work on desensitizing your dog to almost everything they will be coming into contact with in their lives. Another term for this is socializing your pup, but it's more than introducing them to other people or other dogs. Socializing a dog also includes getting them familiar with their environment, the people and things around them, and the sounds they may come in contact with.

How to Do It

1. Expose your dog to different textured floor materials one at a time. Some examples include tile, wood, and grass.
2. If you would like to take this activity a step further, introduce uneven surfaces, such as the woods, sidewalk grates in the city (only if your dog's paws are big enough to not fall through), or a sandy beach.
3. If your dog has mastered all of the previously mentioned floor materials, try this exercise on an escalator and an elevator.

How It Helps

This activity can be done at any dog's age and can be important in building their confidence. Slippery floors or wobbly surfaces can be scary at first! But, with time and patience, your dog can be challenged to face more and more of these materials. Switching up their surroundings to desensitize them to what they encounter in their world is a cheap and easy way to give them some environmental enrichment.

Have a Backyard Treasure Hunt

Backyards can get boring when you see the same thing day in and day out. Make it more fun for your dog with a treasure hunt! The only materials this activity requires are a fenced-in yard or long leash and some strongly scented treats your dog enjoys.

How to Do It

1. Either have someone else hold your dog on a leash or put them in a small area (like an outdoor pen) where they can see you but can't follow you around. You want your dog to know that you are hiding something for them to find.
2. Hide treats all around the fenced-in yard. This can be under leaves, on a branch that your dog can easily access, on a large rock, or on any other feature in your yard that is accessible. Keep track of how many treats you hide so you know when your dog finds them all and the activity can end.
3. Let your dog wander around the yard.
4. If they have trouble finding any treats, help them by showing one of the hiding spots.
5. When all of the treats have been found, be sure to signal the end of the activity by removing your dog from the yard.

How It Helps

The outside world is full of fun smells. Can your dog decipher the smell of their treats from all of the other distractions? Their typical yard is now a fun game of hide-and-seek!

Explore the Object Pile

In this activity, your dog will be experiencing and reacting to different surfaces and objects that they may come to face in their lifetime. This can include things such as rugs, blankets, pillows, chairs, baskets, and whatever else you can think of. In this fun activity, your imagination is the limit! Think creatively and use what you already have in your home. This activity will both enrich your dog and desensitize them to objects that may be a big deal to dogs if they are not introduced at a younger age.

How to Do It

1. Gather all the items you want to use for this activity.
2. Put all of the objects on the floor in a wide-open area that you are comfortable with your dog interacting with. Somewhere with fewer outside distractions is best.
3. Don't be afraid to layer your materials, put things upside down, and generally make it more of an obstacle course for your dog. For example, you can roll a rug into a ball on top of your carpet, then place your kitchen chair upside down on top. Just be wary of creating falling hazards.
4. Add some treats onto your surfaces for your dog to find.
5. Release your pup and let them explore. As always, keep a close watch on them so that they are interacting with the desired objects—not other precious items that may be nearby.
6. The next time you complete the activity, try a rotation of new items that you didn't use during the previous exercise. This will encourage exploration since the items will be new to your dog and will allow you to create an infinite number of object piles for them.

How It Helps

As silly as it may seem, this kind of activity can help to desensitize your dog to materials you may not even realize they need to be desensitized to. It's important for you to try to socialize your dog to their world as much as possible, and this is a fun and easy way to incorporate objects into their world while they find the tasty treats. It's kind of like a giant snuffle mat!

Take a Dip in the Kiddie Pool

Kiddie pools aren't just for your human kids—they're great for your fur babies too! An easily accessible plastic pool can be found at many retailers, and the possibilities for filling them are endless. Your dog is not limited to splashing in water on a warm summer's day. No matter the weather or the season, this enrichment tool can be used all year long, both inside and outside. One day, fill it with water and play outside; the next day, stuff it with blankets and pillows for a comfy snuffle-bed experience.

How to Do It

1. Decide what kind of enrichment tools (ball pit balls, pillows, water, toilet paper rolls, your dog's toys, rolled-up newspaper, etc.) would best fit your dog today. Set up the pool indoors or outdoors based on your decision. If you decide to use water, set it up in an area you're comfortable getting splashed.
2. Fill the pool with the enrichment tools/toys. Feel free to mix up what's in the pool during each iteration of the activity to keep things fun and different.

3. If this is your dog's first encounter with whatever you filled the pool with, start with a slow introduction. Don't force them into the pool—let them check it out at their own pace. You can help to encourage exploration by sprinkling in some treats as well.

4. Take note of what your dog does or doesn't enjoy. Each dog has their own preferences. If they don't like the items you used this time, try a different set of items the next time.

🐾 Pet Pointers 🐾

There are a few different kinds of pools you can purchase. The hard plastic ones are cheap and durable but take up a lot of storage space. There are also foldable PVC pools with drain holes that are more expensive but are easily storable. If filling the pool with water, make sure that your dog's head will always be above the water in case they decide to lie down in it.

How It Helps

When you fill the pool with water, tennis balls, or another item, you allow your dog to interact with a material or substance they may not come in contact with every day. It is in a small, controlled space, and they can investigate it on their own, which can help to build their confidence during new scenarios in the future. It's important to foster your dog's sense of curiosity so they can be confident and comfortable dogs.

Go on a Hike

If you can travel to a mountain or trail, hiking is a great and easy way to incorporate enrichment into your dog's routine. Your hike can be a beginner's hike or a more challenging one, depending on the experience level of you and your pup. A hiking loop does not have to be a steep, rocky climb but can be as simple as a walk through the forest. The main point of this activity is to get your dog into a new environment where they can be challenged physically and mentally.

How to Do It

1. Plan out where you want to go, what loop you want to walk, and what items you may need to bring. This can include some extra snacks and water (with a bowl for your dog) if you plan on going for a longer hike.
2. When going on your hike, be aware of the rules of each individual location. You can typically find this on a park's website or on the trail sign at the beginning of the hike. Some hiking loops may only allow leashed dogs. On these loops, test your pup on a long lead.
3. It may take some time to figure out, but be aware if a hiking loop is busy with many other visitors or if it is typically quiet. Some dogs thrive in quieter environments, while other dogs may enjoy being more social. This will depend on your dog's personality and preference. A dog who is not great around strangers may benefit from a more private space.

4. While hiking, allow your dog to take in the environment around them, which may include walking on the crunchy leaves or sniffing out a good rock. You will want to check in on your dog every few minutes, even if they are on a long leash, to make sure they are not getting into anything they shouldn't. It's also a great chance to work on their recall behavior.

> ### Safety Tip
> Remember that even if a park or trail allows off-leash dog walking, it is a common courtesy to leash your dog when walking by others on the path, especially if the path is narrow. There are many people who may be scared of or allergic to dogs, or they may be walking past with a reactive dog who is in training.

How It Helps

In addition to physically tiring out your dog, a good hike will mentally wear out your dog. Taking in the environment around them, especially a place they do not visit often, takes a lot of energy. Whether your hike is long or short, your pup will constantly be experiencing new or changing sensations throughout your walk.

Have a Sleepover at a Friend's House

Whether your dog is joining you for a sleepover at a friend's house or visiting a friend's home while you're on a weekend vacation, sleeping in a new place can be enriching for dogs who are comfortable with it. This activity is great for dogs who feel secure with other people and who are calm in environments that are not their home.

How to Do It

1. Ask a friend or family member if they are okay with your dog sleeping over at their house.
2. Bring your dog's bed, blankets, or crate to help them feel more relaxed in a new environment.
3. Have the person caring for your dog (or if you're staying over, you) follow the same nightly routine as usual, including feeding time, bedtime, etc.
4. Make sure your dog gets lots of love and attention for showing calm behaviors in their new environment.

🐾 Pet Pointers 🐾

If it's your dog's first time sleeping anywhere besides your home, it may be helpful for you to stay in the same room with them if possible.

How It Helps

This exercise helps your dog to adapt to new environments quickly, which is a learned socialization skill. The new, temporary environment can be enriching to dogs and switches up their routine by physically taking them out of their regular space.

Rotate Nesting Materials

Birds are usually the first animal that come to mind when you think of a nesting animal. But mammals, including your dog, may nest too (even if it's in a slightly different way)! Rotating their bed, blankets, or even an alternative crate switches up your pup's environment.

How to Do It

1. Switch out one item at a time, especially if you have a younger or newly adopted dog since these kinds of dogs are already adapting to their current environment.
2. Rotate items every few weeks and wash them in between switching them.

🐾 Pet Pointers 🐾

Get to know your dog better by taking note of the materials they like better than others and incorporating more of the preferred ones in the future. Make sure that you have multiple types of similar materials to rotate: If you know your dog likes blankets, always include a blanket in their rotation.

How It Helps

Nesting is a normal dog behavior and doesn't need to be discouraged if your dog is doing it safely and with the proper items. When you give your dog a novel item to nest with, they may be more likely to spend more time with it to get their scent on it.

Paddleboard or Kayak

If you live near a body of water or plan on traveling to one soon, this exercise is a great way to incorporate your dog's enrichment into your own fun activities. Kayaking is an activity where you sit down in a boat and paddle using oars. Alternatively, it's safe to take dogs in canoes, which are usually larger and deeper than kayaks, requiring more than one person to paddle them. A paddleboard is a long floating board where you can stand, kneel, or sit while paddling in the water. This activity is best for dogs who can control themselves when around distractions, such as ducks in the water or other boaters in the area, and are comfortable being in or around water.

How to Do It

1. Pick your watercraft of choice, whether a kayak, canoe, or paddleboard. For a first time out on the water with your dog, opt for kayaking or canoeing, as paddleboarding requires even more focus and balance.
2. Get in/on the watercraft first and get your dog in/on with you, letting someone assist you if necessary. Your dog should have enough space to be comfortable either in front of you or behind you. Having your dog on your lap can be dangerous since it prevents movement on your end, which is needed to move the boat or paddleboard.
3. Reinforce where you want your dog to stay on the boat or paddleboard by giving them treats when they stay in the correct spot.
4. Go on your water adventure! Begin with shorter trips, such as five minutes, and work your way up to longer ones if your dog is comfortable.

How It Helps

It's not often that dogs get the experience to be on top of the water, and there are many dogs who enjoy this kind of activity. Some examples of breeds who may enjoy this activity include Labrador Retrievers, Standard Poodles, and Nova Scotia Duck Tolling Retrievers. It not only switches up their everyday routine, but also builds the foundation of trust between you and your dog.

NOTES

NOTES

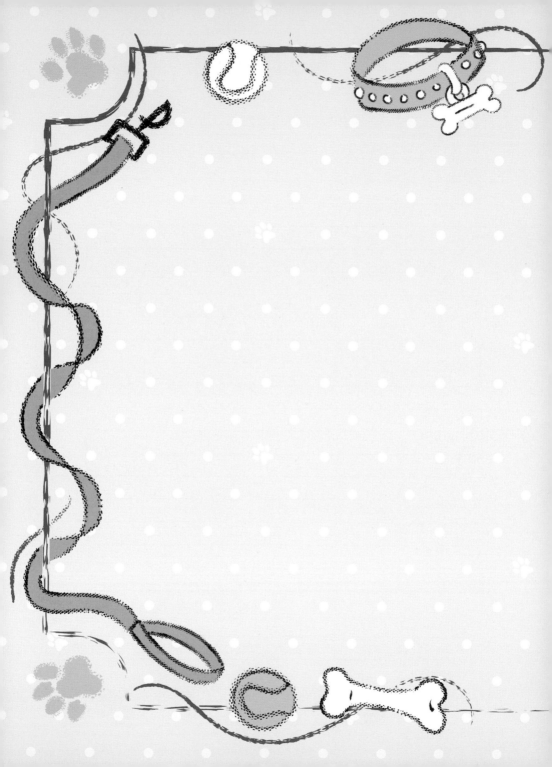

CHAPTER 2
Food Enrichment

There are so many creative and fun ways to feed your pup that will make mealtime more rewarding. You may have heard of the term "ditch the bowl," which means exactly what it sounds like! There are so many different ways to feed your dog without just throwing their kibble in a food dish. This chapter is full of creative activities you can easily implement to feed your dog in a way that challenges their mind and their senses.

Explore Earth's Natural Snuffle Mat

Sometimes the earth naturally provides the best areas for your dog to explore! This activity is mainly for people with grass or clover yards, although you can also do this activity in a public park that you thoroughly check beforehand. If you decide to use any public space, be prepared to inspect the area you will be using for anything nonedible or hazardous, or any food item (natural or human-made) you don't want your dog to eat. Using a natural snuffle mat allows the grass to act as the mat while using your dog's kibble as the treat/incentive for snuffling.

How to Do It

1. Find the space you want to use as your snuffle mat. The smaller the space, the less challenging the activity is. Remember to always start easy and work your way up to a challenge.
2. Scatter your dog's kibble within your chosen area and let your dog sniff out where the food is.
3. Watch your dog find the food throughout the grass. Be wary of other dogs in the area if you are using a public park.

How It Helps

This activity is a free and easy way to switch up your dog's meal. Since dogs are contrafreeloaders, they will love this activity. They not only have to use their senses to find where their food is, but they also get to eat their meal in a completely different environment. The best part is that you can do this activity anywhere there is clean grass!

62 • HAPPY DOG

Play with the Bell Pepper Feeder Toy

Does your dog rip all their feeder toys to pieces? Try this activity instead. Bell peppers are rich in vitamins and antioxidants for your dog, making them a perfect alternative for destructive dogs. Red bell peppers are the best type to use because they have the highest number of vitamins for your dog. They can be carved out to make feeders and can be filled with many other foods, such as peanut butter, kibble, and plain Greek yogurt. Depending on the fillings, you may want to lay out a mat on the floor before your dog starts.

How to Do It

1. Carefully slice the top of the bell pepper off, removing the stem.
2. Remove the seeds from inside the pepper.
3. Add fillings of your choice.
4. Give to your dog. Since everything is edible, don't worry about your dog consuming the entire pepper in one sitting.

How It Helps

There are some dogs who cannot have feeder toys because they will destroy or ingest parts of them. Other dogs may need a switch-up in their routine. This bell pepper feeder toy is a great alternative way to give your dog their meal outside of their bowl or as an afternoon enrichment snack.

Enjoy an Edible Birthday Cake

Although this cake can be used for any special day, this enrichment activity frames this cake as a birthday (or Gotcha Day) cake just for your dog! The best part about this exercise is that you can use any of your dog's favorite foods. Most foods can be shaped in a way to make a special multilayered cake for your dog. Pick up a cupcake if you want something to chow down on, as this one is dog (not human) friendly.

How to Do It

1. The bottom layer of the cake should be sturdy and the largest layer. The easiest way to make this layer is to soak kibble until it is malleable or use your dog's raw food, then use a bowl or round cake pan to shape it into a flat circle, like a layer of a regular cake. It's recommended that you use your dog's meal for this layer to prevent them from overeating during the day. Remember: If you plan on serving this to multiple dogs outside of your fur family, you will need to check in with their parents to verify that your pup's pals have no allergies or sensitivities. Freeze this layer for one to two hours.

2. Once frozen, add a layer of plain Greek yogurt on top of the bottom layer as the icing.

3. For the next layer, get creative by adding an even layer of dog biscuits or round-cut vegetables.

4. Add another thin layer of plain Greek yogurt.

5. Add a few pieces of fruit to the top, such as blueberries, watermelon, or skinned apple.

6. Add an optional edible candle by carving your dog's age out of a large carrot. Be careful during this part! If you're just

looking for a photo opportunity before giving it to your dog, you can also use a regular cake candle (unlit, of course). Just be sure to remove it before letting your dog eat the cake.

7. Give the cake to your dog.

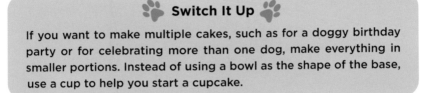

🐾 Switch It Up 🐾

If you want to make multiple cakes, such as for a doggy birthday party or for celebrating more than one dog, make everything in smaller portions. Instead of using a bowl as the shape of the base, use a cup to help you start a cupcake.

How It Helps

This is a fun activity that gives your dog their meal in an unconventional way. Plus, it allows you to have fun and find a delicious (for them!) way to celebrate a special day for your dog. The entire cake is edible so you don't have to worry about your dog ingesting anything they shouldn't, and they can enjoy the special treat while you get some great photo opportunities to show off your masterpiece.

Play the Destructible "Towel" Game

Any true enrichment toy that your dog receives should be okay for them to rip apart. It's part of the territory! Since your pup cannot distinguish between what is okay and what is not okay for them to destroy, be conscious of what you are giving your dog during their enrichment. Fabric is not included in this book because your dog will not be able to distinguish their enrichment towel and your nice guest-room towels. All that said, here is an activity you can give to your dog that mimics a popular enrichment game without the possibility of ingesting fabric or destroying towels around your home.

How to Do It

1. Gather any kraft packing paper you have on hand, whether it's saved from packages you received in the mail or fresh from a roll you bought at the craft store.
2. Roll out 1—2 feet of packing paper. If you're using recycled paper from the mail, spread the paper flat on a table.

Ensure that the recycled paper is free from staples or tape, which are ingestion hazards.

3. Place kibble or dry treats randomly on the piece of packing paper.

4. Start rolling the paper from one corner and roll the paper completely, on a diagonal. Make sure to roll in such a way that all of the treats or food are distributed throughout the roll and not just in one spot.

5. Knot the paper one or two times to make it into a puzzle.

6. Allow your dog to either destroy the packing paper to get to the food or unknot it. Be sure to monitor them as they do this activity—though paper isn't harmful to ingest, you do not want to encourage eating it either.

🐾 Pet Pointers 🐾

Save any packing paper you get from mailed packages or other types of mail. Your future self (and your dog) will thank you! Make sure anything that you save is not a plastic choking hazard for your dog; instead, kraft packing paper or a newspaper will do. The newspaper will be less sturdy.

How It Helps

Because the material in this activity is not harmful if ingested, it is much safer than using a fabric towel. Your dog will have to figure out how to unknot the paper or destroy it to get to the food. You can even use your dog's entire meal in this activity by using a longer piece of packing paper and creating a larger puzzle. Let them shred up their toy and have fun—just be prepared to clean up afterward!

Sniff a Snuffle Mat

One of the more popular enrichment toys out there, a snuffle mat can come in many different sizes and shapes, but the general idea is the same. The mat can be made from rubber or fabric and should have fabric strips to hide food in. A snuffle mat may also have pockets to hide food in as well. Snuffle mats are easy to find online, but your local pet store may also have some in stock if you want to judge what your dog would want in person.

How to Do It

1. Once you have your snuffle mat, add kibble or treats throughout the fabric strips and hiding areas.
2. Create a challenge by burying some food deeper within the mat! Entice your dog to try by hiding some pieces of food that are easy to find.
3. Let your dog sniff it out, but make sure they are having fun. If your dog looks frustrated, help them out!

How It Helps

A snuffle mat is designed to encourage foraging and sniffing, which are both natural canine behaviors. You can use a full meal of kibble in a snuffle mat, eliminating the use of a bowl for a meal. It also entices your dog to work for their meal, encouraging their contra-freeloading behavior.

Introduce Lick Mats

Different than a snuffle mat, have your dog work for their food with this fun enrichment tool! Stores make soft ones, which are better for dogs who have never tried a lick mat or for senior dogs. You can also find durable ones made of thicker silicone that are more challenging. There are also lick mats that have suction cups to stick to flat surfaces, making them perfect for bath time. Lick mats also come in a very difficult bowl shape.

How to Do It

1. Choose the lick mat with an appropriate difficulty.
2. Spread soft, dog-friendly food on the mat. This can be something such as wet dog food, plain Greek yogurt, a squashed banana, or dog-friendly baby food. You can add one food or multiple treats to the mat.
3. Let your dog lick the mat.

> 🐾 **Challenge Accepted** 🐾
>
> To make the lick mat even more challenging, freeze it for a few hours with the food spread on the mat.

How It Helps

Licking is a natural dog behavior that releases endorphins (or the feel-good chemicals) in a dog's brain. It can help to relieve stress and encourage calm behaviors. There is also a large variety of foods you can give to your dog on a lick mat, and the mat can easily travel, making this activity a staple in many enrichment plans.

Play with a Rolling Treat Ball

Does your dog love chasing after balls? If so, this enrichment activity may be perfect for them! Although treat balls can be purchased in different shapes and sizes, they all serve the same purpose: to make your dog work for their food! Your dog must roll the ball around so that the food falls out of the hole, and then they can eat it. This activity can be used as enrichment for a snack or can fully replace an entire meal typically eaten in a bowl. This exercise is a perfect example of contrafreeloading, or making your dog interact and earn their food, instead of simply getting kibble in a bowl. Many dogs prefer this method of eating.

How to Do It

1. Purchase the treat ball of your choosing. It should be the proper size for your dog and should not be a swallowing hazard. If your dog is known for chewing and destroying their toys, make sure you get a heavy-duty ball.

2. Place treats or kibble inside of the ball. Do not overfill; otherwise, treats may not come out as easily. You will also want to put the right sized treats inside of the ball. Adding treats that are larger than the hole will make it much more difficult, if not impossible, for your dog to get to the treats. They might then get frustrated. If you're in doubt, add in training treats, which should work with most rolling treat balls.

3. Give the ball to your dog and let them figure it out. Most dogs will immediately know what to do. That said, it's possible your dog may need some help during the first round of the activity.

4. Once all of the food is eaten, remove the ball from your dog to indicate that the activity is complete.

🐾 **Switch It Up** 🐾

Different treat balls will have different challenges. The simplest challenge is the ball with a hollow inside and a hole. In the next step up, there is a rolling ball that has a maze on the inside, which prevents the treat from coming out easily. Your dog may have a preference depending on how much they like to be challenged.

How It Helps

This exercise is a great way to help dogs who eat too quickly slow down and enjoy their mealtime. It can also prevent bloat, which is possibly fatal. During the first few times your dog completes the activity, they will have to figure out how to get the food out of the ball. After that, they may automatically know how to complete the exercise, but it will still burn off excess energy built up throughout their day. If your dog is the type to need variety while eating, there may be different types/materials of rolling treat balls that you can switch out to keep them engaged.

Use Slow Feeder Bowls

Enrichment can be as simple as switching out your dog's food bowl for another. Slow feeder bowls are great for preventing your dog from ingesting food too quickly and can also trigger their contrafreeloading behaviors. As a reminder, contrafreeloading is a behavior where dogs prefer to work for their food over getting it without any effort. Slow feeder bowls are a simple yet effective way to get your dog to work for their food.

There is no shortage of slow feeder bowls in many different shapes and sizes. If your dog doesn't like the first one you try, they may respond better to another type. If you are unsure if your dog will enjoy slow feeder bowls, many companies make slow feeder inserts that can simply be placed inside of your dog's current food bowl.

How to Do It

1. Purchase a slow feeder bowl of your choice. They can be found at pet stores, home goods stores, and many online retailers. If you have a brachycephalic breed or a breed of dog with a shorter snout, there are companies that make shallow slow feeder bowls to prevent frustration. You may have to try a few different slow feeder bowls before finding the right one that will work for your dog, depending on the height of the bowl and challenge of the feeder.
2. Feed your dog their regular meal in the slow feeder bowl. These bowls work for kibble, wet, and raw food.

How It Helps

Unfortunately, dogs can get bloat from ingesting food too quickly. Bloat, also known as gastric dilatation-volvulus, or GDV, is a condition that happens when a dog's stomach fills with air and cuts off blood flow. It can happen quickly and can be fatal if not treated right away. Thankfully, slow feeder bowls can help immensely to prevent bloat from occurring by slowing down how fast a dog can eat their food.

Dogs are also natural contrafreeloaders. They prefer to work for their food over getting it for free. By making them work for their food without making it too frustrating, you are allowing your dog to be a dog!

Solve the Muffin Tin and Tennis Ball Food Puzzle

Some of the best enrichment activities involve items that you probably have lying around your house. This activity is no different! To complete the muffin tin and tennis ball food puzzle game, you need a regular-sized metal muffin tin (either regular-sized six-muffin or twelve-muffin tins will work), tennis balls, and some dog treats. You can also use your dog's meal for this activity as a bowl replacement.

How to Do It

1. Gather all the items needed for the activity in an area away from your dog, such as a table. This will make the exercise challenging, especially for the first time, since your dog won't know that there are treats at the bottom.
2. Place treats at the bottom of the clean muffin tins. It's up to you if you want to put some in each tin or if you want to pick a few muffin holes to challenge your dog. If your dog is new to this activity, begin with filling each tin. You can also use high-value, scented treats to entice your dog to investigate, such as a hot dog slice or a small piece of cheese.
3. Place the tennis balls on top of the tins so that the treats are concealed.
4. Give your dog the muffin tin with the tennis balls on it. If they are having difficulty figuring it out, help guide them by lifting up a tennis ball and showing the treats underneath. Then let them try the activity by themselves.

You don't have to use just tennis balls for this activity! You can use balls of different sizes and shapes or even other smaller toys to create a fun challenge. By adding different textures, patterns, and colors, you will engage your pup's mind more and tire them out. You can also add in a variety of treats to keep the activity interesting. For example, add in some broccoli, apple slices, small training treats, and a dried slice of sweet potato. This way your dog will get a new flavor and texture as they get to each muffin hole in the tin.

How It Helps

Most dogs are very food motivated, and their sense of smell will easily lead them to where the treats are. This activity creates more of a challenge by asking them to either pick up the ball with their mouth or move it out of the way with their nose or paw. This will stimulate a destruction behavior since they will have to essentially take apart the food puzzle in order to get to the food. By simulating destruction, your dog will be less likely to destroy your favorite new pair of fluffy slippers.

Use Rotational Feeding

Is your dog constantly bored? Switch it up by trying rotational feeding. Rotational feeding is varying the contents of your dog's food and rotating between options. If your dog eats kibble, you could try switching from chicken to lamb to salmon over time. You can also switch food forms, such as adding in wet food or meal toppers. Work with your veterinarian to figure out what specific diets you can rotate between, as this activity may not work for dogs with food allergies.

How to Do It

1. Consult with your veterinarian first to decide which foods to rotate between.
2. Follow the general course of how to switch over diets. This includes adding small amounts of the new food into the older food during mealtime. Over a few days, you can increase the newer food and decrease the amount of older food until your dog is just eating the new food.
3. You can continue to rotate your dog's food under the guidance of your veterinarian.

How It Helps

Although dogs have fewer taste buds than humans do (dogs have 1,700 taste bud receptors, while humans have nine thousand), that doesn't mean you can't switch up their foods every once in a while. Rotational feeding can help you give some variety to your dog in a way that doesn't cost you money. As long as it's done properly, your dog can thrive with food variety.

Try Out Silicone Bowls

If they normally eat every meal out of a metal dish, your dog might be bored of their bowl. Silicone bowls are extremely versatile and can be used in a multitude of settings with different foods. The silicone material is safe for dogs and can be frozen.

How to Do It

1. Pick your silicone bowl. You can also use a regular bowl shape or find one that works as a slow feeder. Some may have ridged obstacles, while others may have different compartments. For this activity, the separate compartment bowls will work best.
2. Fill each compartment with dog-friendly food. You can do all of them with the same food or switch them up to give variety.
3. Give your dog the silicone bowl at room temperature, or freeze it for a few hours to up the challenge.
4. Let them sniff through and enjoy the different foods in the compartments.

🐾 Switch It Up 🐾

Try plain Greek yogurt, single-ingredient and dog-friendly baby food, or water with a piece of fruit/vegetable in each compartment.

How It Helps

In this activity, your dog uses their contrafreeloading skills and works for their food. If you decide to freeze the bowl, they will also lick the frozen food, releasing feel-good chemicals.

Destroy Edible Super Chewer Toys

It is very common for pet parents to be concerned about their fur babies eating the stuffing from destroyed toys. While it is typical for most dogs to grow out of this habit and realize that their toy's stuffing doesn't taste as good as it looks, that is not always the case. There are many dogs who just cannot have stuffed toys. If you have a dog who loves to destroy, this activity is for you! Plus, if your dog eats some vegetables in the process, that's an added benefit.

How to Do It

1. Figure out your dog's preferences for dog-friendly vegetables. This may take trial and error, but you will find their favorites after a few sessions.
2. Gather your choice of dog-friendly and shred-able veggies, such as a head of romaine lettuce, broccoli, or large carrots. While most dogs will not need help figuring out what to do with the vegetable, some dogs may need some encouragement for the first few rounds of this activity. You can entice your dog to interact by tossing the vegetable around like you would with one of their toys, or add a little taste of peanut butter to let them know it's okay to eat.
3. Let your dog shred! If you are worried about cleaning up after this activity, use a designated blanket or kiddie pool, or have your dog do the activity outside.
4. Once your dog is no longer showing interest, remove any remaining shreds of vegetables.

How It Helps

One of the most "problematic" behaviors a dog can have is chewing and destroying items. Thankfully, dogs can have an outlet to destroy without being destructive to your home. Giving your dog the ability to shred, destroy, and potentially consume a food item that will not be harmful to them will prevent them from gnawing on your shoes. While some think that allowing your dog to destroy one item will give them permission to destroy everything, that is not the case. You are simply replacing an unacceptable behavior with an appropriate behavior of destroying and consuming a non-toxic food item.

Play with a Snuffle Ball

Does your pup love their snuffle mat? Try out this fun activity! Snuffle balls are a do-it-yourself project that can be made with a stack of scrap fleece and four zip ties. As an added benefit, they are safe to put in the washing machine to easily clean when your dog inevitably makes the toy dirty.

How to Do It

1. To make the snuffle ball: If you are not using scrap fleece, you will need one to two yards of fleece, depending on how big you want your snuffle ball to be.
2. Make a template by cutting scrap cardboard into a circle. The circle's diameter will depend on how big you want the ball to be. For a small ball, use a diameter of 6 inches; for a

medium ball, use a diameter of 8 inches; and for a large ball, use a diameter of 12 inches.

3. Cut out thirty-two circles using the cardboard template.
4. Fold each circle twice. The first fold will be in half, and the second fold will fold the circle into quarters.
5. Make a small hole in the corner where the folds meet, using a pair of fabric scissors. Repeat for all thirty-one remaining folded circles.
6. Place eight folded circles on each zip tie through the holes you just made.
7. Thread the tapered end of the zip tie into the square notch to lock it in place and create a closed loop. Thread the remaining zip ties one by one onto each other so they connect. Once all are connected, tighten the zip ties.
8. Cut off the remaining ends of the zip ties and sand the cut-off edge so it is no longer sharp. Fluff up the ball so the folds are more open and hide the zip tie center.
9. To play: Hide treats within the fleece folds and give the toy to your dog.

How It Helps

The snuffle ball can be used to give your dog a snack, or it can also be used with kibble during your dog's mealtime. It's a very flexible enrichment tool! During play, your pup has to sniff out and manipulate the toy to get to their food, which takes physical and mental exertion to finish. Some clever dogs may even shake the ball to get the food out.

Eat Banana Ice Cream

Making this treat for your dog is perfect for a hot summer day (or night). Bananas are a great treat because they are a good source of vitamins and nutrients that dogs need. All you need for banana ice cream is half of a frozen banana and a blender.

How to Do It

1. Freeze a banana for a few hours. Make sure to peel the banana first—once the peel is frozen, it is more difficult to remove. Preportion the banana into halves before freezing.
2. After your banana is frozen, throw it in a blender. Because the portion is small, personal blenders are generally easier to use, but a regular blender will also work just fine.
3. Blend until the banana creates an ice cream consistency. Typically, this will take a few minutes.
4. For some added fun, add on shredded carrot "sprinkles" or carob chips, which are safe for dogs to consume.

How It Helps

Banana ice cream is a great way to get your dog involved in family ice cream nights, and these sweet treats are even yummy for humans! Because this ice cream is a normal treat given in an abnormal way, this is a perfect example of food enrichment. Banana ice cream is fun for the whole family.

Experience the Egg Carton Game

This enrichment activity is not only fun for your dog; it also allows you to reuse old egg cartoons! As long as they are clean and free of any raw egg, cardboard egg cartons can become a great game for your dog. So, even if you don't immediately use an egg carton, save it for a rainy day.

How to Do It

1. When you are ready to use your egg carton, fill each space with either kibble or another snack.
2. Close the egg carton and give it to your dog. If it is their first time completing this exercise, you may have to help them to open the carton or give it to them unopened.

> 🐾 **Challenge Accepted** 🐾
>
> Add newspaper or packing paper on top of the treats to make this activity more challenging.

How It Helps

Is your pup up to the challenge of puzzling through this egg carton? They not only have to work for their food, but they may also have to destroy the carton to get to the food. This makes it perfect for dogs who like to chew and destroy while also allowing them to use their contrafreeloading skills.

Try Scatter Feeding

Scatter feeding is the act of distributing your dog's food all around a room or an area. It is a really easy but effective way to ditch the regular bowl and challenge your pup's eating rituals. In fact, you don't need any type of bowl for this enrichment activity! It will not only challenge their mind, but will also get them running around the room to find their food. This activity works best if your dog eats kibble, unless you thoroughly clean the room each time before and after scattering any type of wet or raw dog food. You can also use training treats if you want to make this a quick activity.

How to Do It

1. Place your dog in another room or area. When you are just starting out with this activity, you can show your dog what you are doing. To increase the difficulty of this activity, put them in an area where they can't see you.
2. Scatter their kibble throughout a safe and clean area in your home. For an easier activity, place all food in plain sight. Hide the food behind objects or under easily moved items for more of a challenge.
3. When the food is ready to be found, let your dog into the area.
4. If your dog is struggling to find some food, simply show them where the food is. If your dog is continually struggling, make a note for next time to take a step back and decrease the level of difficulty of the activity. Maybe your dog needs to watch you place it.

How It Helps

This type of feeding exercise is often seen being done by zookeepers because it challenges the animal mentally and is very easy to implement on the caretaker's end. It also mimics what animals do in the wild. For example, wolves would need to smell out and search for their prey because, unfortunately, their food is not as easy to access as it is for domestic dogs today! By completing this exercise, dogs need to use their senses to find every piece and are encouraged to use their natural behaviors to work for their food. You may be surprised just how tired your dog is at the end of this activity.

Play with an Edible Apple Feeder Toy

Feeder toys that can be stuffed with food, such as peanut butter or wet dog food, are typically made of rubber, but sometimes it's fun to change things up! Grab an apple from your kitchen and get creative. Put the apple to good use by DIY-ing a toy for your dog. This way they have some variety in their day-to-day activities.

How to Do It

1. Take an apple and make sure it is mold-free. A general rule of thumb is if the dog-friendly food item is good enough for you to eat, then your dog can eat it. However, you will want to do some quick online research to confirm this before giving your dog anything new.
2. Peel the skin off of the apple. Depending on the dog, apple peels have the potential to cause digestive upset due to their fiber content.
3. Spoon out the apple core. Generally, it is easier to spoon out from the top so that you can easily remove the stem and get out all of the apple seeds. Apple seeds contain cyanide and can be harmful if ingested in large quantities.
4. Once you have your apple feeder toy, fill the hole with any dog-friendly food your dog enjoys. Try peanut butter, a handful of your dog's kibble, or a spoonful of plain Greek yogurt.

Pet Pointers

While dogs can eat any type of apple, go with apples that have the most crunch to get the most out of your dog's apple feeder toy. Typical crisp apple types include Honeycrisp, Pink Lady, and Fuji apples.

How It Helps

The edible apple feeder toy is an excellent way to present food to your dog in a novel way. Most dog toys are either inedible but challenge your dog's brain or are edible but are not as challenging. In this do-it-yourself project, your dog can eat the entire apple, and it will challenge them to get all the delicious food on the inside. Your dog also has the option to shred the apple if they don't love the taste, which simulates the destructive behavior in an acceptable way.

Try a Rapid-Fire Mealtime

Rapid-fire mealtime is another great way to give your dog their food without using a bowl. It is easily done by firing out your dog's kibble one or two at a time. This is a great rainy-day activity that just uses the meal your dog receives every day. However, if your dog eats wet or raw dog food, you can use small treats for this activity and make it a shorter duration to prevent overeating. This exercise is also a great way to expel extra energy or get low-energy dogs moving more.

How to Do It

1. Measure out the amount of food for your dog's meal. You can choose to start with a portion of your dog's meal and work up to their full meal after a few sessions. If you're using treats, start with a few and work your way up to a small handful.
2. When both you and your dog are ready, throw a few kibbles or treats away from you so your dog can see where they land.
3. When your dog returns to you after eating the kibble from the floor, throw out more. You can increase the challenge here by throwing kibble in different directions each time, making sure your dog can reach the area it is thrown. One piece of kibble can be thrown down the hall, and when your dog returns, you can throw the next one into the kitchen.
4. Repeat until the meal is finished or you have run out of treats.

How It Helps

This activity requires both mental and physical exercise for your pup! Not only will your dog have to run back and forth, but they will also have to use their senses (sight, smell, and sound) to figure out exactly where the food landed. It can help slow your dog's eating habits and provide a fun bonding activity between you and your dog. You might be surprised (and happy!) by how tired out your dog is at the end of this exercise. It's a great way to tire out your dog for the morning before going to the office or running some errands. It's also a fantastic exercise for rainy days when you can't get outside and your dog has excess energy.

Introduce the Bowl Smorgasbord

You don't always have to ditch the bowl to give your dog some food enrichment. In fact, this exercise encourages bowls—lots of them! The bowl smorgasbord includes dividing up your dog's food into two or more bowls. For example, put some food in their regular bowl, with the rest of their food in a slow feeder bowl. Maybe you have some heavy-duty plastic bowls to throw into the mix too. Use what you have to make it fun.

How to Do It

1. Gather the bowls you want to use with the food your dog will receive as their meal. It's up to you if you want to evenly distribute among the bowls or if you want to do it unevenly. Add a little peanut butter, plain Greek yogurt, or banana to a bowl for a welcome surprise.
2. Divide up the food into the different bowls.
3. Set the bowls down and let your dog eat.

How It Helps

Observe which bowl your dog eats from first. This is a good opportunity to see contrafreeloading in action. As a reminder, contrafreeloading is when dogs prefer to work for their food versus getting it for free when they are given the option to choose. Does your dog eat from the slow feeder bowl first?

In this activity, your dog has freedom of choice, which is incredibly important in enrichment. In addition to showing you which bowls they prefer to eat from, this activity may decrease stress and burn some energy.

NOTES

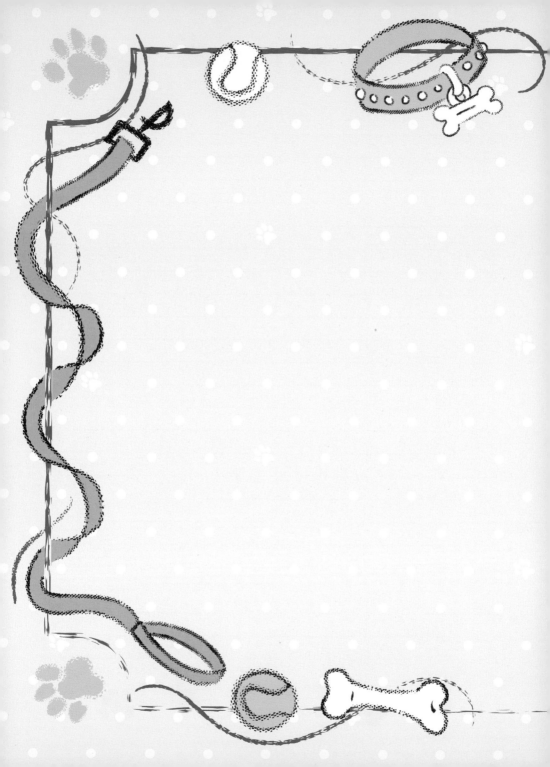

CHAPTER 3

Sensory Enrichment

Think of the five senses: sight, sound, taste, smell, and touch. The senses that dogs use the most in their daily lives are their senses of smell and sound. And, of course, they experience these senses in a much different way than humans do. If you put your dog's senses to the test with these enrichment activities, you will end the day with a tired, happy dog!

Play Seasonal Games

Depending on where you are in the world, you can take advantage of the seasons as they change. Each season brings something new and exciting! With these exercises, you can enrich your dog's senses while only using a favorite toy and the nature around you. Since these activities depend on the time of year, your pup will experience new things as the seasons rotate, but fall and winter will work best for this exercise. Remember that dogs can see blue and yellow best, so start out with a toy of those colors.

How to Do It

1. If doing this activity in the fall, rake up some leaves into a pile. If doing this activity in the winter, wait until you have a decent amount of snow and shovel the snow into a pile. In spring or summer, you may have to improvise with stacking twigs or grass clippings.
2. Grab one of your dog's favorite bright-colored toys.
3. Start a game of fetch with your dog by throwing their toy into the pile of leaves or snow.
4. Continue until your dog loses interest in the game.

How It Helps

Both leaves and snow are enriching to your dog's senses since they have such a different feel than the textures they may normally walk on. Freshly fallen leaves or snow may also have different smells than they are used to, and when you throw their toy into the pile, your pup will rely on their nose and eyes to find the toy.

Use Dog-Safe Scents

What's actually safe for your dog to sniff or ingest? Sometimes even naturally occurring fruits or other plants can make your dog really ill! This is also true of essential oils. While there are many essential oils that are dangerous to dogs in any form, all essential oils can be dangerous if ingested in their undiluted

form. Thankfully, there are many ways you can enrich your dog with natural scents. Some of these dog-friendly scents include ginger, mint leaves (except for English pennyroyal, which is toxic to dogs), cinnamon sticks, basil, and rosemary. You can use any of these for this fun sensory challenge!

How to Do It

1. Decide which scent you want to try with your dog. It's good to have a couple on hand before you start this activity.
2. See if your dog likes the scent you've chosen first by offering them the scent and watching their reaction. If they're interested, they will show it by continuing to smell the scent, and if they don't enjoy the scent, they will back away or make a scrunched face.

3. If in an outdoor area, you can rub the scent on rocks, out-door chairs, a stair, or any other object where your dog has easy access. The outdoors likely has more changing scents over time, so this might make the difficulty of the challenge slightly higher.

4. If indoors, you can rub some of the scent on a plastic toy, a piece of paper towel, or cardboard. Only rub the scent on things your dog can inspect closely with their nose.

5. Allow your dog to smell the scent until they lose interest.

6. If you used a plastic toy, wash the toy off with soap and water when the activity is complete.

Safety Tip

All of these examples are nontoxic to dogs in small amounts and should not be used excessively.

How It Helps

There are so many ways to enrich your dog's sense of smell using products you may already have in your pantry! By using food items, you also don't have to worry if an essential oil will cause harm to them. You can use these safe scents for different enrichment activities to get your dog's brain (and nose) going.

Freeze a Hol-ee Roller Ball

This activity is great to beat the summer heat! Not only can the exercise cool your furry friend down; it also occupies them for an extended period of time. For this exercise, all you will need is a Hol-ee Roller ball, water, and a plastic zip bag big enough to fit the ball in, and it's optional to include a plastic cup. The Hol-ee Roller ball is a dog toy made of a durable rubber that has holes and allows you to fill it with many options, including treats, other toys, or, in this case, ice. They come in many sizes, so be sure to get one that makes sense for your dog. They also come in varying levels of durability. While the original Hol-ee Roller ball is very durable, it may not stand up to strong chewers. However, there is a Hol-ee Roller ball with even stronger rubber for the dogs who need it.

How to Do It

1. Place the Hol-ee Roller ball inside of the plastic zip bag. If using a plastic cup, place the ball in the bag on top of the cup.
2. Fill the bag with water just enough to cover the ball.
3. Shape the bag around the ball so that the water will freeze in a round shape.
4. Bunch the bag up at the top of the ball and close off with a rubber band.
5. Place in the freezer until the water is frozen.
6. Once frozen, remove the bag and give it to your dog in an outdoor area that you don't mind getting wet. Your dog may lick the ice and play with the Hol-ee Roller until it melts. The ice "cubes" will come off of the ball as they play.

How It Helps

This activity is super easy and customizable to what your dog enjoys. You can keep them intrigued with the ball by adding some of their favorite snacks while cooling them off during hot days. This is also a great time to try out some new foods that are safe for your dog, such as nutritional vegetables like carrots. Adding them to the ice in the Hol-ee Roller ball will make it more exciting for your dog to try. The ice will also enrich their senses, making it a great exercise that you can prepare ahead of time before a busy week.

Listen to Music

Did you know that the type of music you play for your dog can actually have an effect on their mood? Studies have shown that dogs have their own taste in the music that they hear! Typically, heavy metal music made dogs agitated and resulted in barking, while classical music was shown to have a calming effect. So, it's better to play your pooch some soothing lullabies or light-spirited folk music before bedtime. This activity also might be great for calming anxious dogs before leaving for a few hours or before you anticipate loud noises outside (such as construction or a firework show).

How to Do It

1. Find a classical music playlist wherever you listen to music, whether it be through a musical subscription service or on a free online platform. You can play it on your phone through a speaker, or you can find channels on your television to play.

2. This activity can be unsupervised since it is proven that classical music encourages calm behaviors. If you decide to play another type of music, supervise your dog to see their reaction to it. Calm behaviors you will want to look out for include floppy, relaxed ears and no facial tension in their mouth or eyes. Start the volume low and work your way up to a comfortable level.

3. Switch up the playlists throughout the week. This will not only give you a chance to see your dog's different reactions and learn more about your dog's personality; it will also switch up your dog's routine while enriching their sense of hearing.

How It Helps

Classical music can be played during a time when your dog may be stressed, such as when fireworks are going off near your home or during a thunderstorm. The calming tunes will not only help promote relaxed behaviors, but can also be a good distraction during a stressful time. Putting on a playlist, even during times that are not stressful, will be enriching for your pooch's senses. It's also a great chance to learn about your dog's personality. Do they prefer rock over reggae?

Use Old Clothes

One of a dog's keenest senses is their sense of smell. It's amazing that your pup can decipher your scent as their pet parent versus that of a stranger! Studies have even proven that dogs show positive associations with the scent of their owner as compared with other scents. Plus, they prefer human scents over other dogs' scents. This enrichment exercise is super simple and helps keep up that positive association.

How to Do It

1. Grab a worn T-shirt, sweater, or sweatshirt that you don't want to wear anymore. Cut off any tags and remove any lace/strings that your dog would pull at.
2. Put the item of clothing in their crate or on their bed.

How It Helps

Putting a clothing item where your dog spends their day or night will not only enrich their sense of smell; it may also help them to relax and de-stress. It can also help your dog bond to you through your smell. This is a great exercise for pet parents welcoming a new furry addition to their home.

Introduce a Babble Ball

A Babble Ball is a specific type of ball made for dogs that makes all sorts of noises as a dog rolls it around. There are some that make random noises, others may make animal noises, or there are some that speak short sentences. Any of these can make great enrichment activities for your dog that don't include your close participation. Plus, it's great for your hyperactive pup and can give you a break from the traditional game of fetch!

How to Do It

1. Decide which type of Babble Ball to use. If your dog has a favorite sound, search for a ball that makes that sound.
2. Give the ball to your dog and watch their reactions to the sounds. They should be intrigued and excited by the ball, not scared of it. You may need to try more than one ball!
3. Remove the ball once your dog loses interest in it.

How It Helps

Dogs love squeaky toys because they imitate the sound of prey. Babble Balls have a similar effect. A Babble Ball should keep your dog engaged in play and enrich their senses through sound.

Play Snow Hide-and-Seek

If you live in an area that gets lots of snow during the winter months, you have a great opportunity to vary your playtime and enrichment activities! Playing hide-and-seek with your dog's toys in the snow is not only an activity they don't get to do most days, but it also encourages them to use their senses to find the toy in the snow. Make sure that your dog is in a fenced-in area or that they have been trained well with recall. You can also use a long leash for this activity if your dog needs it.

How to Do It

1. Although you don't have to wait for the snow to completely stop falling, you will want to wait long enough so that there are a few inches of snow on the ground to use for this activity.
2. Grab one or two brightly colored toys to play with. You will want ones that are very visible so that you can easily find them in the snow if your dog can't. If you want them to pop for your dog, pick blue or yellow toys. This way they will stand out in the snow.
3. Head out either to your yard or to an area where you won't get many distractions from other people or dogs. This activity is not advisable in a public park, for example.
4. For at least the first few rounds of play, show your dog where you are hiding the toys in the snow.
5. Let your dog find the toy and bring it back to you.
6. Repeat the activity for a few rounds until you're cold or your dog is bored and/or tired.

How It Helps

Snow is most likely something your dog does not experience in their everyday life; however, most dogs love playing in it! This activity is a great way to incorporate your dog's toys into an exercise that allows them to do a little bit more, such as digging for the toy or sniffing out the toy in the snow. If you work up to the challenge of not showing your dog where the toy is in the snow, it provides an additional challenge that will tire them out even more.

Pop and Play with Bubbles

Everyone seems to love bubbles! This includes your furry four-legged friends. What's not to love? They are shiny, float, and are super satisfying to pop. While there are bubbles that are specific for dogs (that are typically bacon or peanut butter flavored) and can be ingested, you can also use child-friendly bubbles! With the child-friendly variety, just make sure you prevent your  dog from ingesting them. Eating the soapy liquid may cause an upset stomach or other digestion issues. If they happen to ingest some of the bubbles, be sure to give your dog plenty of water to drink and watch them for any vomiting.

How to Do It

1. Pick whichever bubble mix you would like to use. If you are worried about your dog ingesting the bubbles and are looking for more of a food-friendly activity, choose the dog-friendly, edible variety of bubbles.
2. This activity will require less cleanup if done outside. The dog bubbles are sticky when they pop on the ground and will need to be mopped up if you decide to complete the activity indoors.

3. Allow your dog to be curious about the bubbles. Some dogs like to pop the bubbles with their mouths—if your dog is curious and mouthy, it's safer to get the dog-friendly bubbles. Other dogs may enjoy observing them more than popping them. In these cases, child-friendly bubbles are totally appropriate.

🐾 Challenge Accepted 🐾

If you are looking to up the challenge, make this activity into a game! Use the edible bubbles and blow one bubble at a time. Only blow the next bubble when your dog catches it or when it hits the ground if your dog misses it.

How It Helps

Bubbles are certainly something your dog is not likely to run into often. They are typically used during special occasions, so your dog may have never seen them before. It's reasonable that your dog may be hesitant to interact with them at first. If you get flavored bubbles, these bubbles may also have a scent to them. (Make sure they do not try to slurp up the liquid bubbles before they are blown!) The popping sensation of a bubble is also a new sensation to most dogs as well—it's a new way to play.

Experiment with Noise Desensitization

Desensitization is the process of helping your dog to become less sensitive to a stimulus. For example, many dogs are scared of fireworks during the Fourth of July or New Year's Eve due to the overwhelming sound. Dogs' ears are generally much more sensitive than a human's, so the big bursts of sound are not just startling but probably terrifying. Noise desensitization can be done all year-round to help your dog become less sensitive to those loud sounds during those special occasions when they might hear them. This is also a good enrichment activity since you can make it into a positive experience, and the sounds you expose them to are usually things that they don't hear every day.

How to Do It

1. Pick one noise that your dog is sensitive to, such as fireworks, thunderstorms, or a fire truck alarm. You will likely know which of these sounds your pup has problems with, but if not, experiment a little. Don't overwhelm your dog with loud sounds. Start at a low volume and watch for pinned ears, which means your dog is frightened.
2. Search for the sound online. Many videos you will find have these sounds on repeat so that you can work with your dog for a few minutes.
3. Play the problematic sound on a low volume when your dog is in a calm state.
4. Praise your dog for staying calm and relaxed.

5. Start with this activity lasting only a few minutes on a low volume in the beginning. As your dog becomes more comfortable and stays in a calm state, you can increase the duration and volume of the sound. Eventually, they should barely react to the activity.

> ### 🐾 Pet Pointers 🐾
>
> **If you find your dog is tense or uncomfortable, lower the volume more and slowly work your way up to a higher volume. This may take a few sessions, so be patient. You want to be on the lookout for calm body language, such as soft, squinting eyes and loose, relaxed movements, which will show you that your dog is comfortable.**

How It Helps

During this exercise, your dog is working on their sense of hearing. This activity is full of sounds that they don't hear in their everyday life. Over time, they will become less sensitive to the sounds, which is the main goal. To switch things up for you and your pup, you don't always have to do sounds they may dislike, but you can also do other sounds they may enjoy or are indifferent to that they don't hear all the time, such as birds chittering or people having conversations.

Eat Dinner in the Park

Dinner in the park is a low-impact exercise that is perfect for senior dogs as well as puppies who need to learn impulse control. That said, this activity can also be great for almost any dog who needs a change of scenery once in a while. Plus, it has the added benefit of being simple to set up for, though it requires a quick walk or drive to your nearest park. This activity allows your dog to eat their dinner away from other dogs and people, but these distractions will still be close enough for your pup to observe.

How to Do It

1. Pick your favorite park or spot outside. Once you're there, make sure that there is a space for you to sit with your dog, preferably putting a distance between you and any crowds/other dogs and dog owners. This will allow you to build up a relationship where your dog will focus more on you and their dinner over other dogs or people.

2. Allow your dog to eat and observe their environment in your chosen spot. It may be best to keep them on-leash if you are unsure if they will wander off.

3. Ask your dog for their attention every so often during this activity. You can start by asking them to look in your direction and build up to having them make eye contact with you to focus. Reward your dog every time they look at you.

4. Once your pup finishes their meal, you can walk around the park or head home.

How It Helps

Eating dinner in the park can engage your dog's senses, and it's obviously a big change in their routine and environment. Your dog will also have the chance to observe other dogs and people from a distance, which can help you immensely with reactivity training. It can also help with getting your dog to focus on you. This activity may even stimulate low-energy or elderly dogs enough to take a nap when they get home.

Start a Rock Collection

Calling all geologists! Your dog (and you) will love starting an out-door rock collection. But how does this activity challenge your pups? It's estimated that a dog's sense of smell is thousands of times better than a human's. While people take in the world mainly visually, dogs take in the world and gain perception through scent. So as bizarre as this activity may seem, it has a purpose that you may not find useful for yourself. This activity includes collecting rocks from outside of your backyard and placing them in your backyard. By making sure they're from another environment, they get lots of great new-to-your-dog smells.

How to Do It

1. While out on a walk somewhere new or a little farther out-side of your typical neighborhood, with your dog or by yourself, collect any rocks that catch your eye (or your dog's nose).
2. Place them around your yard if you have one, or if you live in an apartment, make a designated spot in your home, and switch them out occasionally.

How It Helps

Think of how rocks are interacted with in their environments. Each pebble could have scents from other animals. No matter what, a stone from the park will always have a different smell than your backyard. Your dog may be out in the yard one day, sniffing the usual smells, and then come across a new rock with all kinds of new scents. Your dog will then try to figure out what those smells are.

Go on a Scent Stroll

Different types of walks will engage your pup's brain in different ways. So how about a scent stroll? This activity is ideal in open, quiet, and clean environments where your dog can be on a long lead (a really long leash). Between 30 and 50 feet is ideal for a scent stroll.

How to Do It

1. Find the area that you want your dog to explore. The perfect situation would include a quiet but spacious area where your dog can explore uninterrupted by others.
2. While your dog is on the long leash, allow them to sniff wherever they want to go. This activity encourages giving your dog freedom to roam.
3. Because your dog is still on a leash, you can easily get control of them if they are in a stressful situation.
4. Give them fifteen to twenty minutes of sniffing time.

> ### 🐾 Pet Pointers 🐾
> Sniffing for about twenty minutes can be equally as tiring as an hour-long walk, and this activity requires much less effort on your end.

How It Helps

Enrichment is not only about getting out excess energy mentally and physically; it is also about giving your dog autonomy and the ability to de-stress. This activity is a low-impact and easy way to let your dog be a dog! The ability to sniff is essential to a dog, and a scent stroll is helpful after a day inside.

Switch Up Your Teatime

It's difficult to find scents to use for enrichment that don't contain any chemicals and are dog friendly. However, you may be surprised by how easy it is to make a sensory activity for your pup at home! One of the easiest and most convenient ways to incorporate natural scents into your pup's enrichment activities without any mess is to utilize some of the tea bags you may already have in your pantry. Some teas that may work for your dog include mint, ginger, lavender, and turmeric. Dogs—like humans—have their own preferences in smells.

How to Do It

1. Find a tea bag that your dog enjoys. You can quickly figure this out by offering it to your dog for them to smell. Watch their behaviors. If they continually smell it and don't walk away or scrunch up their muzzle, they most likely tolerate

(or even like) the scent. Try out different teas to gauge their reactions.

2. Take the preferred tea bag to a clean room without many other smell-filled distractions, like food. Hide the tea bag in an area where your dog can sniff out and maneuver to. If you want to up the challenge, you can hide the tea bag in a paper bag, which will create a slight smell barrier between the tea bag and your dog.

3. Watching your dog carefully, give them some time to track down the tea bag.

4. Once they find the tea bag, reward your dog with a treat. You can then take the tea bag away and either try the activity again or put it away for another day.

🐾 Pet Pointers 🐾

If you don't have any single-bagged teas in your home that are dog friendly, you may load loose-leaf tea into a metal or rubber tea-steeping device. Make sure it is properly closed, and closely monitor your dog during this activity—they may mistake this for a toy. You can test this out before starting. Your dog should be more interested in the smell of the tea than the steeping device.

How It Helps

Allowing a dog to sniff burns more energy than you may think! After a few rounds of this activity, they may be ready for a nap. Also, using a tea bag means you don't have to worry about any hazardous materials from inside the bag, and the convenient packaging prevents any mess during this activity. That said, if you have a dog who likes to shred paper, watch them carefully throughout this exercise.

Make a Frozen Pup-Sicle

During hot summer months, everyone needs some time to cool off! What better way to turn down your pup's body temperature than by offering them an icy homemade treat? Creating a frozen pup-sicle for your dog is simple and easy. All you need to complete this enrichment activity is a hard plastic or paper cup, water, and some cut-up fruits or vegetables.

How to Do It

1. Gather all of your supplies. If your dog has not received this enrichment before, use fruits or vegetables that you know they like. That way they will be actively trying to engage with their frozen treat. After this activity has been completed two to three times, add in some new foods for your dog to sample.

2. Fill the cup with as much water as you think your dog will enjoy. The bigger you make it (the more water you use), the more challenging the activity. So, for the first couple of times, you may want to use less water. This will also be dependent on the size of your dog. If you have a smaller breed dog, such as a Yorkshire Terrier, make the pup-sicle smaller, and if you have an extra-large breed, such as a Newfoundland, you should make the pup-sicle larger to prevent creating a possible choking hazard.

3. Place the fruits or vegetables in the water. Try out different dog-friendly foods to see what floats and what sinks. This will create an even dispersal of food throughout the pup-sicle.

4. Place the cup inside your freezer for at least two hours so that it freezes completely.

5. Once completely frozen, remove the pup-sicle from the cup. If you're using a paper cup, you can tear the paper away from the frozen pup-sicle. If you're using a hard plastic cup and are finding it difficult to separate the ice from the cup, run the outside of the cup under warm water until the ice pops out.

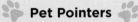

Pet Pointers

There are many options for additional foods you can add to your pup-sicle. For example, blueberries are full of healthy nutrients and sink to the bottom, while lettuce shreds float in water. You can also add in bone broth for some added nutrients. Avoid foods that are unsafe for dogs, including grapes, lemons, tomatoes, or cherries.

How It Helps

In addition to being an effective way to cool off on those really hot days, this activity is a great sensory experience for dogs. Most dogs enjoy ice cubes, but the additional challenge of licking until the ice melts to get the food inside makes the experience different and more exciting. Only give your dog their frozen treat in an area you don't mind them getting wet.

Watch Some Dog-Friendly Television

It's hard to believe, but there are hundreds of videos out there on the Internet that are made for one audience and one audience only: dogs. Whether your dog enjoys bird-watching, looking at scenic ocean views, or following a stroll through the woods, there's a television show (or online video) out there for your dog. There are both free and paid versions of these shows for you to pick from, and this activity can be a great way to occupy your dog while you're in a work meeting.

During the first few sessions of doing this activity with your dog, you should watch them very closely. While curiosity is certainly encouraged, there will be some dogs who may be reactive or act negatively toward certain elements of the videos you put on. Be on the lookout for raised hackles (the fur along their backbone), growling, barking, or any other signs of frustration, which will tell you that it's time to turn off the television or find another video. It may take some time to figure out your dog's preferences on the videos they watch.

How to Do It

1. Either sign up for the paid version of television for dogs or find your chosen video playlist for free on the Internet.
2. Pick the show you think your dog may enjoy. Some dogs may bark at other dogs on-screen but be fine with watching a forest scene—your dog will have their preferences, just as you do.
3. Let your dog watch the show.

How It Helps

These videos made specifically for dogs are a unique way to immerse your pup into a new environment. For example, maybe your dog has never been to the beach before. A beach-themed video lets them experience the look and sound of the waves. Or maybe your dog relaxes as they watch birds fly by, but you're unable to see as many during winter months. There's a video for that too! These dog-friendly shows are typically appealing to dogs because they usually showcase the colors that dogs can see best.

Have Fun with Pumpkins

As seasons change, your dog misses out on many of the year-round festivities. Thankfully, there are lots of ways you can celebrate the seasons with your dog. One way is with pumpkins! Take a couple precautions before giving a pumpkin to your pup and while they play. First, cut off the stem: The stem is prickly and can cause digestive upset if ingested. Second, observe their play carefully: Raw pumpkin skin can also cause stomach upset for some dogs because of the high fiber content. So, the pumpkin can be shredded for this activity but should not be ingested.

How to Do It

1. While any size of pumpkin can be given to your dog, a small- to medium-sized pumpkin is best. Make sure the pumpkin is big enough that it's not a choking hazard.
2. Carve the pumpkin to remove the stem, pulp, and raw seeds. Small amounts of cooked pumpkin seeds without spices are safe for your dog to ingest as a seasonal treat.
3. Once carved, add some treats to the inside of the pumpkin so that treats fall out when your dog rolls it around. Watch them shred and interact with the pumpkin, taking it away if they try to eat it.

How It Helps

The act of shredding is a natural behavior for dogs. Most dogs love having the chance and choice to destroy. When you put treats into a pumpkin as well, it adds another enticing component. It also allows your dog to join in on the autumn festivities!

Listen to the Radio or a Podcast

Looking for an easy way to entertain your dog? Just turn on your favorite radio station or podcast! This is a great example of passive enrichment, or enrichment that doesn't require any physical energy from your dog. Plus, it's super easy for you as well. This activity is perfect for enriching your pup while you're out of the house because it involves minimal supervision. It's a win-win situation!

How to Do It

1. This activity requires minimal effort to set up. Turn on the radio or podcast on your phone or speaker at a normal level (whatever is comfortable and relaxing for your pooch to listen to).
2. Play the music for a few minutes or queue up some to last a couple of hours.

How It Helps

Dogs can hear nearly four times better than humans. Listening to different tones of voices, laughs, and even the occasional jingle in between sets of a podcast or radio show is a form of sensory enrichment that works your dog's sense of hearing and challenges their attentiveness. This activity can also help to de-stress dogs from noises they hear outside their home, whether it be the mail carrier or your neighbor's construction. If they have a radio show or a podcast to listen to instead, it can help them focus energy on other tasks.

NOTES

NOTES

CHAPTER 4
Cognitive Enrichment

Though humans and dogs are different in many ways, after a long day of using your brain, you're tired! It takes a lot of energy to solve problems, and this form of enrichment is called cognitive enrichment. These cognitive-focused activities include ways to make your dog puzzle over how they're going to get to their food or take in the environment around them. Training sessions are also common in this category, which is both enriching and helpful for your daily life.

Solve a Cutting Board Treat Puzzle

Your dog will appreciate this homemade puzzle that is perfect for enrichment. In order for your dog to do this activity, you will first need to complete a simple do-it-yourself project. All you need for this puzzle is a new BPA-free plastic cutting board (pick one that's thick and doesn't bend), a drill, cotton twine, sandpaper, and some of your dog's treats. For treats, you will want small training treats, xylitol-free peanut butter, and jerky strips.

The premise of this activity is to create a hanging board that will be drilled with holes to fit delicious treats. Your dog will interact with the puzzle in order to get to the treats.

How to Do It

1. To construct the puzzle, you will need to use different-sized drill bits to drill holes of varying sizes throughout the cutting board. You may want to put a scrap piece of wood underneath the cutting board so that you do not drill into the surface below your project. Be sure to make each hole big enough to fit a treat. Model your holes after your treats. For example, for a small, round training treat, make sure it can fill the hole so that it won't fall through. If you make bigger holes, you can also use peanut butter to help the treats stay in place.
2. Drill one hole (big enough to fit the cotton twine through) in two adjacent corners.
3. Thread 2 feet of cotton twine into the two holes and knot to create a hanging board. This is necessary so that your dog can interact with the board upright.
4. Use the sandpaper to smooth down all of the holes. If the holes are not smooth, they may injure your dog as they play. Then, the base of your puzzle is complete!

5. To play this activity: Fill the holes in with training treats, jerky treats, and peanut butter.

6. Hang the board, and let your dog figure out how to get the treats.

🐾 **Pet Pointers** 🐾

Pick the size of your cutting board that will work for your dog. A small-sized cutting board, such as an 8" × 10" board, works for most small and medium breeds as well as puppies and senior dogs. More active or larger breeds can use a 10" × 14" or even an 18" × 24" cutting board.

How It Helps

Fun fact: This exercise is actually adapted from a zoo enrichment activity! Plus, you may notice that this puzzle is similar to a lick mat, except the board is hanging and the treats are stuck inside of the drilled holes, making it more of a challenge for your dog. Your pup may have to use their mouth, tongue, or paw to finish the cutting board treat puzzle.

Figure Out a Pool Noodle Puzzle

Looking to upcycle some old, weathered pool noodles? This DIY activity is fun and gives your old stuff a new purpose. For this activity, you will need one pool noodle, one large cardboard box, and some kibble or your dog's favorite treats. Your pup will have to figure out how to get around the pool noodles to get the treats at the bottom of the box.

How to Do It

1. Cut the pool noodle a little longer than the width of the box. Cut at least two pieces of the pool noodle, but use more if your box is large.
2. Cut pool noodle–sized holes in both sides of the box so that the noodles fit through the width of the box. Repeat for the other piece of pool noodle.
3. Place both pool noodles into their holes, place the treats on the inside of the box, and let your dog get the treats at the bottom.
4. Supervise your dog to ensure they don't accidentally get their head stuck between pool noodles.

How It Helps

This is an easy food puzzle you can create at home using simple items. Your dog will have to process how they can get to the treats while facing an item they don't run into every day.

Give Each Toy a Name

This exercise is a low-impact activity that takes a lot of brain power from your dog. When you give each toy a name, your dog will puzzle over giving you the correct one.

How to Do It

1. Grab one of your dog's favorite toys.
2. Name the toy and place it down in front of your dog.
3. Say the name of the toy and reward your dog when they pick up the toy after you say the name. If they don't get it right away, you may have to start rewarding them for something simpler, such as looking at the toy.
4. Repeat and practice.

> ### 🐾 Challenge Accepted 🐾
> Once your dog has mastered the toy's name, place it next to another item, such as a pillow, and ask your dog for the toy again. See if they can still distinguish between the two.

How It Helps

This activity can help to prevent boredom since you can practice this skill multiple times a day. It's an easy and cute enrichment activity, and your friends will love telling your dog to "get Panda" from the other room! As your dog increases their skills in distinguishing individual toys, you can add more to your repertoire.

Play the Three Cups Treat Game

Ready to test your dog's intelligence? Though not the only way to test your pup, this way might be the most fun and delicious. To play, this easy game needs two types of simple objects that you already have in your home: three cups or bowls and some of your dog's favorite treats. Plastic or nonbreakable bowls and cups are preferable for this exercise where you will be shifting them around in front of your furry friend.

How to Do It

1. Gather the objects needed to complete the game.
2. Find a flat surface in your home or outside that your dog can easily access. This can be on a shorter table or hardwood or tile flooring. You want the cups to be able to move around easily without lifting them off the ground.
3. Turn all of the cups upside down and place in a horizontal line next to each other.
4. Place one treat or piece of kibble under one of the upside-down cups, and let your dog see which cup you put it under.

5. Switch the cups up without lifting them or revealing where the treat is.

6. After moving the cups around, let your dog guess which treat the cup is under. They may do this by nosing or pawing the cup.

7. Reveal to them if they were correct! If they guessed correctly, let them have the treat.

8. If they guessed incorrectly, take away the incorrect cup and let them guess again to try to get the treat.

9. Repeat as often as your dog is interested in the game.

🐾 Challenge Accepted 🐾

To make this game easier, use two cups instead of three. This will give them better odds of picking the correct cup. If your dog is ready for more of a challenge, use five cups and place one treat under one of the cups.

How It Helps

Puzzles like this can help to challenge your dog mentally in ways they probably haven't tried before. They are challenged to use their intelligence and also their sense of smell to try to find the treat the fastest way (finding the correct cup). Repeat this activity to see if your dog gets faster at the puzzle!

Play with a Water Bottle Rattle

This activity requires you to construct the rattle first, but thankfully it's an easy process. Plus, the sound and feel of the toy is great for a high-energy pup. You will need a plastic water bottle, a scrap of fleece (at least 18" Ð 12"), and some of your dog's favorite treats. These materials will become a rattle toy for your dog that will also dispense treats. What a great combination!

How to Do It

1. To construct the rattle: Lay the piece of fleece flat length-wise. If it is not already, cut it to 18" Ð 12".
2. Cut 1" slits every inch on both sides of the fleece, totaling eleven cuts per side. You will be cutting on the 12" sides.
3. Place the water bottle lengthwise on one end of the 18" sides as close to the middle as you can. The top and bottom of the bottle should each be facing the cut slits you just made.
4. Wrap the water bottle in the fleece so the cut slits are still on the top and bottom of the bottle. The fleece should be covering the entire bottle.
5. Insert your dog's favorite treats into the water bottle. They should be small enough to easily fall out of the bottle.
6. Knot all the cut slits so the water bottle will not fall out, but there should still be some room at the top of the bottle so that the treats can fall out as your dog plays with the toy. You can do this by not knotting the slits too tightly.

7. To play with the rattle: Give the toy to your dog to destroy. If they are confused by the toy at first, roll it around a little for them to disperse a treat. Once they understand how it works, continue to monitor them.

> ### 🐾 Pet Pointers 🐾
> This toy is not meant to last more than one or two sessions. If your dog destroys it, replace the bottle for the next round. If the fleece stays intact, feel free to continue to use it. Wash it in between uses.

How It Helps

This easy, do-it-yourself toy makes enticing noises with the crinkle from the water bottle as well as the treats tumbling around inside. It also challenges your dog to figure out how they can get to the treats on the inside, whether it's finding out how to unknot it, shaking it around until the treats pop out, or using their nose to dig the water bottle out from inside the fleece. You may even be able to fit your dog's meal of kibble in the water bottle to replace their bowl at dinnertime.

Train in Random Intervals

An interval is a space in time between events. When you apply that definition to this activity, it means that you will pick a random time in your day to train with your dog. Build no schedule—it can come as a complete surprise to your dog when it happens.

How to Do It

1. Pick one or two behaviors you want to work on with your dog, such as sit, down, stay, or wait. You can start working on new behaviors or brush up on some old ones.
2. Sprinkle in training sessions of about five minutes each throughout your day.
3. Use training treats during your session to keep your dog interested.

How It Helps

Random interval training sessions help keep your dog on their toes. They will never know when training sessions (and some fun treats) are coming next! This activity also gets your dog to use their brain more often than conducting one longer training session during your day. So, if you do it long enough, they will be challenged through-out the day and tired by bedtime.

Find the Sound

Dogs take in their world around them through their senses. Even though it is not considered their strongest sense, sound is an important way your dog makes sense of their environment. In this activity, you will use intriguing sounds, and your dog will try to find where they are coming from.

How to Do It

1. Find a video or sound clip of sounds dogs love on an online streaming service on your phone.
2. Once you have the video picked, hide your phone in another room away from your dog or under a blanket.
3. Play the video loud enough so your dog can hear it.
4. Let them find your phone and treat them when they find it.

> **🐾 Pet Pointers 🐾**
>
> **Your dog may be interested in some sounds more than others. Try animal sounds, squeaky toys, or sirens to get started.**

How It Helps

This exercise will work your dog's senses a fun new way. Since they cannot use their other senses to find the phone, they will have to tune in to the sound in order to find it. While this activity is best suited for dogs who can hear, you can modify the exercise for deaf dogs by setting your phone to vibrate, placing the phone on a surface that can vibrate, such as a hardwood floor, and letting your dog complete the activity.

Engage with a Cup Tower

Timber! This destructive cup game will be a great way to get your dog's urges to destroy things out in a productive and fun way. You will be building a stacked cup tower for your dog to deconstruct. This activity requires treats or kibble and three to ten cups. These cups can be paper if you want this activity to be destructive, or they can be plastic, as long as you pick cups that you are okay with getting damaged or scuffed up. Different cups will also change the level of challenge of this exercise. Paper cups will be easier to tear apart to get to the treats, while sturdier plastic will challenge your dog to take the cups apart to get to the treats.

How to Do It

1. Pick out the cups that you want to use and your kibble. A lesser number of cups will be easier for dogs who have not done this activity before, and adding more cups will increase the intensity of the challenge. The size of the cups should always be large enough so your dog doesn't get their muzzle stuck in them, and they should all be the same size.
2. Start with your first cup and add some kibble to it.
3. Add another cup into the first cup. Note that you are not making a triangular tower of cups but placing one cup inside of another to create a linear tower.
4. Repeat adding kibble into the cups until you have used all your cups.
5. Give the cup tower to your dog. If you give them plastic cups, be sure to watch for any plastic pieces that may break off during the fun. Make sure that you are monitoring your dog so that they do not ingest any inedible items.

How It Helps

During this activity, dogs must use their thinking skills to find how to deconstruct the cup tower to get the food inside. They may use their teeth, their nose, or their paws to get the cups apart from one another. If you decide to only put kibble in some of the cups instead of all of them, your dog will also have to figure out which cups to go after to get the maximum reward in the shortest amount of time. If you use paper cups, tearing up the cups will replicate the natural behavior of destroying, which is great for dogs who go out of their way to find items to tear apart.

Play a Game of Chase

One of a dog's favorite activities (depending on the dog, of course) is to chase. Most dogs have a prey drive, or just want to stick close to their human, which will motivate them in this exercise. This activity is challenging both mentally and physically. It is also an important training tool that will help you to build trust in the relationship with your dog. If your dog learns to play chase with you, it can also help if your dog gets off-leash and you need to get them to a safe area.

How to Do It

1. Find an area where your dog can run freely. Options can include a fenced-in yard or a distraction-free public area where your dog can be on a long lead.
2. Start running away from your dog.
3. Encourage your dog to follow you. If you're just beginning this exercise, you can reward your dog with treats when they get to you. As your dog becomes more familiar with the activity, the game of chase itself is oftentimes rewarding enough.
4. This activity is great for puppies who haven't learned to follow you yet and love to run off, but it is also a great exercise for older dogs who simply need to get their energy out.

> **Safety Tip**
>
> It's important to never chase after your dog; they should always be chasing after you instead. If your dog learns that it's fun to be chased, this can lead to issues where they may think that you trying to get them out of an emergency situation is actually you asking to play a game of you chasing them, which can lead to unfortunate circumstances, like your dog running out into the road.

How It Helps

The skill in this activity can help in emergencies where your dog suffers from a lack of recall skill. This exercise can teach them to look to you and that you should be their focus. Most dogs love to chase, and this gives them an outlet to do it safely. Be on the look-out for overstimulation behaviors, such as a rapid heart rate when the activity is not currently happening, nipping, or being hypervigilant, where your dog may get too excited during the activity, which means you should have a time-out so your dog can relax and calm down. If your dog is overstimulated on a consistent basis, it can lead to compulsive behaviors, such as tail biting or constant licking, or possibly reactivity in the future. Just as it's important for your dog to learn how to play properly, it's also important for them to learn how and when to rest. That's where it's your job to step in and tell them when an activity is done.

Learn with Recall Tag

Recall tag is not only a great way to get some energy out of your dog; it also strengthens your dog's recall behavior, which is extremely important in your everyday lives. Recall is the behavior of your dog returning to you when they are called, even if there are distractions in the area. It is a very necessary skill for your dog, especially if they pull away from you on a busy street or chase after a squirrel in the woods. This behavior takes practice and time to perfect, but when you make this task into a game, it's fun not only for your dog but also for you!

How to Do It

1. You need two or more people for this game, training treats, your dog, and a large space, ideally an enclosed outdoor space, although this game can also be played inside.
2. Spread out as far as you want to go. Keep in mind that it may be easiest to start at a shorter distance if you have a dog who has never played the game before, a senior dog, or a small dog.
3. One at a time, have each person call out your dog's name and the cue you have decided to use for recall. This can be a word, such as "come," or you can also use a whistle for recall. If you decide to use a whistle, only use that specific whistle for dog training to prevent confusion. Once your dog runs to the person who called them, have them reward your dog with a small training treat, and then have someone else call your dog's name.
4. Start off with short sessions, and gradually increase the duration over time.

How It Helps

This game is a great combination of physical and mental exercise. Not only does your dog have to run from person to person, but they also have to know their recall behavior, what the behavior means, and who cued the behavior. Feel free to incorporate this exercise into your daily routine to continue to strengthen your dog's recall. Play the game in your backyard, in a friend's house, or at a local, dog-friendly park where your dog can be off-leash or on a long leash. With a lot of practice and time, recall will be second nature to your dog.

Dig Through a Surprise Bucket

Does your pup really like going through the trash, or maybe their toy bin, rifling through the different scents, tastes, and textures? Do they like a little mystery when they are out and about for their daily strolls? If so, this activity is perfect for them! Putting together a surprise bucket will allow them to explore in a controlled environment. For this activity, you will need a bucket, some packing paper, and treats or kibble. You can use something as small as a children's beach bucket, a hardware store's gallon bucket, or something as large as a tote bucket. This will depend on the size of your dog. A large tote bucket will not work with small dogs, just like a child's bucket will not work with extra-large breeds.

How to Do It

1. With a bucket sized appropriately for your dog picked out, place treats or kibble at the bottom. The best way to figure out what size will work for your dog is by making sure

your dog can't get their head stuck in the bucket and that there's plenty of room.

2. Cover the treats with crumpled-up packing paper. You can also add some treats to the crumpled packing paper itself.

3. Give the bucket to your dog and let them sniff it out. Monitor them so that they do not ingest a lot of their bucket's components—paper is not an edible snack for them to fill up on.

Challenge Accepted

Increase the challenge by adding in distractions, such as tennis balls, their favorite toys, and other kinds of paper (such as printer paper) or by adding an easily removable cover on top of the bucket.

How It Helps

Your dog may have seen these items separately around your house and not thought much of them. When you put them all together in an enrichment activity, they take on a whole new life. Your dog has to think critically to find where the treats or kibble are hidden within the bucket and packing paper. Plus, they have the added enrichment of the sounds of the paper crinkling as they dig through their bucket. If you added additional challenges, such as toys or a cover, they have to figure out to look beyond those to find the real hidden goodies within the activity.

Play the Object Permanence Game

Does your dog have object permanence? Object permanence is a psychological concept that an object still exists, even if you can't see where it went. For example, if your dog's ball rolls under the couch, you know that the ball didn't just disappear. Human babies don't understand object permanence until they grow older. That said, studies have found that canines have similar object permanence to one- to two-year-old children. You can test your pup with this enrichment activity!

How to Do It

1. Collect three cardboard boxes and use an unscented toy.
2. While your dog is in the room, show them which box you place the toy in.
3. Remove your dog from the room and bring them back in.
4. Let your dog find the toy.

> ### 🐾 Pet Pointers 🐾
> **Using an unscented toy will mostly prevent your dog from relying on their sense of smell to find the toy.**

How It Helps

Could your dog find the toy on the first try? If they went right for the correct box, then they most likely have some object permanence. This is a fun exercise to get to know your dog and how they see the world around them. It also helps to challenge them mentally to see if they can figure the game out.

Guess the Hand Treat Game

Enrichment activities can be really easy! You can get your dog thinking with only your hands and some smelly treats. You can do this activity with multiple people as well, which will make it more challenging for your dog to figure out.

How to Do It

1. Without revealing the treat to your dog (you can simply place your hands behind your back), put one treat in one of your hands and close your fist.
2. Once the treat is secure in your hand, show both of your closed fists to your dog.
3. Let them guess which one the treat is in.

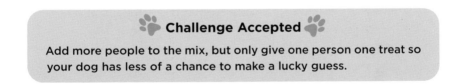

🐾 Challenge Accepted 🐾

Add more people to the mix, but only give one person one treat so your dog has less of a chance to make a lucky guess.

How It Helps

During this activity, your dog will not know automatically which hand the treat is in. They have to use their focus and senses to figure out the puzzle. It's low-effort and can be done for as many rounds as you want.

Use a Homemade PVC Toy

Have some extra construction supplies around? Maybe a PVC tube or two? PVC is a type of plastic tubing that can easily be found and purchased at a home improvement store. It is very durable and great for destructive dogs because it is not easily destroyed. Though it will take some work to construct, you will end up with a toy that can be used consistently. Once created, you can add treats or small toys inside the PVC tube, and your dog will have to roll the toy around to get whatever is on the inside.

How to Do It

1. To make the toy: When purchasing, you can cut the PVC to size while at the store or have an employee do it for you. Get at least 12 inches of PVC tubing for this activity, but if you have a large or extra-large dog, buy a longer tube.
2. You will also need to purchase two fittings that are equal to the diameter of PVC you purchased. One will be a regular PVC cap, and the other will be a threaded PVC cap. These will cover the ends of the tubing and prevent treats from rolling out. The threaded cap will allow you to screw the cap on and off, which will make it easier to add in treats or smaller toys.
3. Use drill bits to drill holes into the PVC tubing and create holes all over the tubing. Make sure the holes are big enough for food, treats, or small toys to fit through.
4. Sand down the holes so there are no sharp pieces of plastic surrounding the drilled holes.
5. Add the PVC cap to one end.

6. To play: Add treats, kibble, or small toys into the PVC tubing.
7. Screw on the threaded cap to the other end of the tubing.
8. Give it to your dog to figure out how to get the food or toys out.

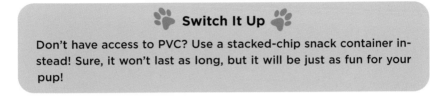

🐾 **Switch It Up** 🐾

Don't have access to PVC? Use a stacked-chip snack container instead! Sure, it won't last as long, but it will be just as fun for your pup!

How It Helps

Dogs have a natural curiosity to them and will typically use their nose or paws to investigate. This activity will spark their curiosity but also allow them to be a little rougher because of how durable the material is. They will have to use their cognitive skills to figure out how exactly to get the snacks out of the holes.

Play Hide-and-Seek

Building your trust and communication skills with your dog is as important as keeping them physically fit! Playing hide-and-seek with your dog is a great way to strengthen your bond and challenge their senses. This game is best played indoors with two people, or you can play alone with your dog if they have a good sit-stay cue.

How to Do It

1. Have your dog sit-stay, or have another person distract your dog so they can't see where you're going.

2. Find a good hiding place. Make it easy if your dog has never played before, and up the challenge as your dog begins to understand the game. You may want to hide behind a chair in the next room for an easy hiding spot and upgrade to hiding in an upstairs closet for a harder challenge, for example.

3. Once you have your hiding spot, call your dog's name or use their release command to let them out of their sit-stay, and then stay as quiet as possible.

4. Let your dog try to find you on their own. Call their name again if your dog can't find you after a minute. You don't want the game to become frustrating for them.

5. Continue until they find you. When they find you, reward with a treat or a lot of praise.

Challenge Accepted

To up the challenge even more in this activity, do it outside! With a much bigger space, it will take a lot more concentration for your dog to find your hiding spot.

How It Helps

This game is a great bonding activity for you and your dog while also reinforcing their recall behavior. Your dog is most likely excited to try to find you, especially if they get treats out of it. This activity also challenges their senses and thinking by making them use their sense of smell to sniff you out, their hearing to see if they can hear you, and their brain to think of where you could possibly be in the house. Remember: After a few rounds, they may be tired—so watch out for a change in their energy level. Otherwise, you may be asking them to find you when they're taking a snooze on their dog bed.

Find the Toy

Find the toy is a game of hide-and-seek using one of your dog's favorite toys. They will use a combination of their senses in order to find a favorite toy and get the added benefit of lots of praise when they locate their toy. It is a great rainy-day activity that requires no real setting up, crafting, or money. Use their favorite toy to excite them for this fun exercise. You can make this activity easier or more challenging depending on your dog's preferences.

How to Do It

1. Pick out one of your dog's toys. For example, you can use a favored plush toy that will have their scent on it, making it easier to find. To extend the activity, you can use a brand-new toy so when your dog finds it, they can then play with it as a reward.

2. Find a hiding spot you want to use that is accessible to your dog.

3. If your dog has not completed the activity before, let them see where you are hiding the toy. However, you will want to have them wait until you hide it before letting them get the toy. For dogs who have done the exercise before, either close the door behind you when hiding the toy or make sure your dog stays in another room while you hide it.

4. Once the toy is hidden, encourage your dog to seek out the toy. They may need some help during the first few rounds of hide-and-seek. You can do this by standing near where you hid the toy, pointing to it, or touching the area where you hid it to help guide them.

5. Praise them and act excited when they find the toy and complete the exercise.

🐾 **Challenge Accepted** 🐾

Make this activity more challenging by hiding in a place that can be easily accessed by your dog but is in a space that they wouldn't normally check. For example, this can be behind a couch cushion or on top of their food storage bin.

How It Helps

This kind of activity strengthens your dog's sense of curiosity and encourages them to use their senses to find one of their favorite toys. Your dog has to think about where the toy could possibly be, and since it is hidden, they also need to process how they can get to the toy. This exercise may take some practice for many dogs. Who knows? Maybe one day, your dog will be able to help you find a lost item with their new set of skills!

Go for a Training Walk

Did you know there are a ton of different types of walks you can take your dog on? A training walk is one great option! This walk has a purpose: to work on two to three of your dog's behaviors. Practicing too many behaviors can get confusing and create frustration on your dog's end, which is why sticking to a few behaviors will work best.

How to Do It

1. Gather all the necessary items for a regular walk, plus a training pouch or fanny pack to carry training treats.
2. Decide on your walking path. Stick to a typical walk you would go on since a newer route would be more exciting and distracting to your dog.
3. As you proceed on your walk, cue the behaviors you chose in the beginning and scatter them throughout your walk. This is a great time to work on your dog's behaviors around distractions, such as another dog walking by or seeing children playing in their yards.

How It Helps

This activity helps with your training plan and bonding with your dog, and it also challenges their brain while providing physical exercise. During a typical walk, they can just go about their business, but during a training walk, they have to think about the cue, remember the behavior, and perform the action.

NOTES

CHAPTER 5

Social Enrichment

Dogs have social lives too! They may get mopey when they don't have enough exposure to the outside world or other people/animals. While it's contested whether or not dogs are pack animals, they are social animals and have the ability to form bonds with their humans, other dogs, and other kinds of animals. These social activities explore your dog's social skills and allow them to expand their community.

Make a Video Call

Similar to TV for dogs, your dog may be more excited by what's on a screen than by your friend's dog. So, maybe you'll have an adorable instance of your pup hopping into your video call with a friend or family member. It may be more difficult for your dog to see the other person, especially on a phone, but they can typically hear and understand the audio.

How to Do It

1. Call up a friend or family member, ideally on a laptop with a large enough screen for your dog to see (if they're interested).
2. Allow your dog to hang out in the call with you or just be in the room while on the call.

How It Helps

This type of activity is passive in that it does not require your dog to exert any energy into the exercise, but they can still benefit from it. It's a win-win for your pup and your grandma or friend! Your pooch may recognize the voice on the other end, and although it does not replace in-person interaction, this is a great supplemental social activity to enrich your dog.

Use a Mirror

Dogs don't use mirrors the same way that humans use mirrors. When a person looks into a mirror, they see their reflection and know that the reflection is an image of themselves. Dogs do not have that recognition of self. Pups will see their reflection as another dog. Some dogs may greet the "other" dog with happy, playful postures, while others might raise their hackles and possibly growl. These are all normal responses, but look for friendly reactions if you want to do this activity with your pup.

While you can use any regular mirror for this activity, you can also purchase an acrylic mirror just for your dog. These mirrors are more shatter-resistant than a typical glass mirror and can be portable, allowing you to complete this exercise from anywhere!

How to Do It

1. All you need for this activity is a mirror. Locate a mirror or other reflective surface that can be placed at your dog's height. They should be able to see at least their face in the reflection.

2. Watch how your dog reacts and remove them from the situation if they get too excited or too stressed.

> ### 🐾 Pet Pointers 🐾
>
> Dogs may show their curiosity by watching and observing the mirror, moving around, or touching their nose to the mirror. Watch out for raised hackles, growling, or lip licking, which are signs of stress.

How It Helps

Even if your dog is not seeing an actual different dog, they think that they are. Since dogs are social creatures, even observing another dog can be enriching for them. After a period of time, your dog may become habituated to the mirror that they may see every day. To switch things up, you can repeat this enrichment activity with different mirrors in different locations. You can also set up the portable acrylic mirror in different locations outside of your home as well. Having these different reflective surfaces in places your dog does not expect keeps the activity fresh. As with many other enrichment activities, it's not wise to continue this activity multiple days in a row—they may tire of it and disengage from the activity.

Go for a Run

Going for a run can be both physically and mentally rewarding for your dog. Plus, this activity gives them a chance to bond with you. Running can be worked up to after your dog masters loose-leash walking and focusing on you versus other distractions, such as squirrels that may run by. This will keep you and your dog safe during the run. You should also consider your dog's breed and age. Some dogs may enjoy running more than others. Breeds to consider skipping a jog with include brachycephalic breeds, such as Bulldogs, Pugs, and Boxers. These pups will have a harder time breathing during the exercise, unfortunately. Since puppies are still growing, most veterinarians recommend waiting until your dog is a year and a half before taking them on a jog, although you can speak to your own vet to confirm.

How to Do It

1. Grab your dog's leash, a collar or harness, and your own running gear and a water bottle. Run during ideal weather conditions to prevent heat exhaustion. Depending on where you live, this may differ. You don't want it to be too hot out, which can give your dog heat exhaustion or hurt their paw pads on the hot ground. Generally speaking, the ideal temperature to run with your dog is between 40°F–60°F.
2. Start in bursts to teach your dog that you will be running. You can also add in a verbal cue to let them know it's time to start moving faster. Go back and forth between walking and jogging.
3. Work on your dog focusing on you rather than what's around them to help strengthen your bond and trust. Start to

lengthen the time period you run for over a few weeks, and soon you will be able to jog with them for your full workout.

> ### 🐾 Safety Tip 🐾
> Avoid using a retractable leash to prevent any injuries to yourself or your dog. Retractable leashes give you less control of your dog and can get caught around your hands or legs if your dog goes running after a squirrel or another dog.

How It Helps

Enriching your dog socially can mean spending quality time just between you and your dog. By changing up their environment and giving them a new activity that they can join you on, you can grow your relationship. Plus, many dogs love spending time outside, moving their legs. It's a win-win situation for them. If you want to be even more social, you can join a local dog-friendly 5K run, where your dog can not only meet other dogs and people but can also join you on your run.

Learn to Rest

Have you ever felt grumpy because you've been moving all day without a chance to sit and relax, even for a few minutes? Dogs can feel the same way! Being overtired can lead to an unhappy pup and an exhausted pet parent. On average, an adult dog will spend half of their day sleeping, 20 percent of their day being active, and about 30 percent of their day being awake, but relaxing. During this 30 percent, learning how to rest is just as vital of a skill as it is for a dog to know how to play. In this exercise, your dog will not only be enriched; they will also be able to master this skill, which they can take with them for the rest of their lives.

How to Do It

1. Bring out a mat, blanket, or bed that will only be used for your dog. If they already have one of these that they are comfortable sitting and resting on, this is ideal.
2. Sit on a chair next to the mat and prompt your dog to lie on it.
3. Reward your dog for lying down on the mat and showing calm behaviors.
4. If your dog continues to lie on the mat, continue to reward.
5. Work up to spacing out the time in between the food rewards.
6. As your dog starts to understand, add in a verbal cue, such as "place" or "go to your mat."

7. You can start to increase the challenge by getting up from your chair and walking around or doing chores, all while asking your dog to stay on their mat.

8. At the end of the relaxation session, you should release them from their mat by saying a phrase, such as "all done."

🐾 **Pet Pointers** 🐾

If your dog won't lie on the mat just yet but will sit on it, reward and work up to the lying behavior. Once your dog understands that sitting and staying on the mat equals treats, they will better understand in the future when you ask them to lie down on the mat.

How It Helps

In this activity, you will be rewarding calm behaviors and showing your dog what you want them to do. This is enriching to your dog because they are still focusing on a task at hand: to stay on their mat. This is a skill that needs to be learned and can help them to further build their social skills, helping them to adapt to environments where they may need to show calm behaviors. Mastering this skill will be particularly useful when people come to visit, you're at a dog-friendly coffee shop, or you're in the middle of a work meeting over video call.

Bring Your Dog Shopping

There are many dog-friendly stores that will welcome both you and your dog! Some of these include Bass Pro Shops, Tractor Supply Company, Petco, or PetSmart. You can always call ahead to make sure your specific store does allow dogs, as some locations may not. When bringing your dog to a dog-friendly store, it is still important to remember proper etiquette and to always respect working service dogs. Do not let your dog approach a working dog. Your dog should also have some basic obedience down before adventuring out to a store, such as paying attention to you and being comfortable on a leash. Though it might be challenging to leave your puppy home while you run errands at dog-friendly stores, be realistic—they might not be up for it just yet!

How to Do It

1. Decide which store you would like to visit, and call ahead to confirm that dogs are allowed if needed. If you want to spoil your dog even more, take them to a store where you can pick up a fun toy for after the activity.

2. Bring some high-reward treats as well as a water bowl if you are going to be out for more than an hour. Having treats easily accessible in a training pouch that sits at your hip is helpful while shopping since you will always have a reward ready to go for your dog's calm behavior.

3. Practice some basic behaviors while in the store to help you generalize your dog's skills.

4. If you're going to stores during a slow period, you can work on socializing your dog to different environments and saying hello to the employees. If you're shopping during a

high-traffic time, you can work on socializing your dog to being calm around strangers.

5. Start with shorter trips to the shops and work your way up to longer time periods if your dog shows calm behaviors.

How It Helps

The ability to go shopping with your dog is a great privilege to take advantage of, as long as it's done responsibly. If your dog is up for the challenge, socializing your dog to many different environments and people is a great step up from them consistently being surrounded by family and close friends. It can help them to generalize their skills, strengthen your training foundation, and help to shape your newest shopping buddy!

Take a Joyride

A joyride is something as simple as hopping in the car and driving around your neighborhood, or you can adventure off to visit someplace new. This activity is perfect for senior dogs who may have a harder time moving around, for dogs who recently had surgery and can't run around, and for newer puppies who need to expel some extra energy and get used to being in the car. Not every dog loves riding in the car, unfortunately, and you will need to watch them to make sure they are having a good time!

How to Do It

1. For this activity, you will need access to a car where your dog can comfortably fit in the back. Make sure they have enough room to move around (they should be able to stand, sit, and lie down comfortably) and are strapped in with a dog-safe leash buckle attached to a harness.

2. Decide on where you want to go. This can be a quick five-minute ride through your local neighborhood, or you can increase the duration and go somewhere farther away. If your dog is new to a joyride, work your way up to a longer duration. Consider giving them treats and praise as they get into the car as a way to ease them into it. The best way to do this is to have two people in the car. While one person drives, the other one can check in on your dog and hand out treats throughout the ride.

3. If you are comfortable enough, your dog has their leash buckle on, and you are going slow enough down local streets, you can open their window and give them a choice to poke their head out. Going too fast can be detrimental to their eyes if something gets in them.

How It Helps

Dogs are constantly taking in the world around them through their sense of smell. When you are able to get your dog out of the house and into an environment where the smells are constantly changing, it can really work their nose. Just imagine the drool-inducing scents your dog may get on a summer day as you pass a barbecue at your local park. This activity is a simple (and practically free) way to work your dog's senses in a low-impact way.

Spend Intentional One-on-One Time

Bonding with your dog is so important! Spending intentional time, even just a few minutes a day, with your dog can be beneficial to both you and your dog's mental health. Bonding with them can build your foundation of trust, which can help during training sessions and can create a relaxed home environment. All you need for this activity is yourself and your dog.

How to Do It

1. Put away your laptop and phone, and turn off your television.
2. Create the time to spend with your dog with no other distractions.
3. If your dog is allowed on furniture, cuddle with them on the couch. If not, spend some time sitting on the floor with them. Be aware of not invading their safe areas without permission, such as sitting on their bed or favorite blanket if they are protective of those things.
4. Use this time to figure out what your dog likes. Do they enjoy being petted, or do they just want to cuddle up to you? This is the perfect time to learn their likes and dislikes.

How It Helps

Because dogs are domesticated, they bond with humans more than their wolf ancestors ever did. It's very important for them to have that opportunity to build bonds and trust with their pet parent. This social activity helps to facilitate the foundation building.

Hang Out with a Stuffed Animal Friend

When a dog is reactive, sometimes being around another dog can cause more stress than not, which is not a goal you want to achieve in enrichment. One way to combat this while still allowing your dog to be socially enriched is to use a stuffed animal. It can be of another dog or another animal. Nowadays, there are stuffed animals that are warm and have a simulated heartbeat to mimic a real dog, which in turn can help calm anxious dogs.

How to Do It

1. Decide which stuffed animal you want to use for your dog.
2. Set out the stuffed animal near your dog. Watch their reactions from a distance. This type of activity can last as long as needed.

How It Helps

Sometimes you don't have access to another dog, but your dog's favorite stuffed bear is in the other room. Even though the stuffed animal isn't real, it has characteristics that can mimic a real animal's and give your dog the social interaction they are looking for. Dogs, at the end of the day, are animals that are naturally used to being in the presence of other dogs. This activity can also give your dog social interaction without stressing them out or otherwise upsetting them.

Watch the World

As simple as it may seem, looking out a window at the world is a low-impact enrichment activity. The best part is that you can have your dog complete this exercise virtually anywhere, whether it's in your own home, at a friend's house, or somewhere totally new. Depending on what's going on at the time outside the window, it can be a relaxing activity or an exciting one. Maybe your pup is watching a group of squirrels zip from one tree to another, they see a friend coming home from a walk, they smell your neighbor's barbecue going, or they are just listening to the wind blow through the trees. You never know what will catch their attention!

How to Do It

1. Pick a window for your dog to watch out of. A window near the front of your house may show some people or other dogs walking by, while a window near the back of your home may be more relaxing with birds and white noise.
2. Entice your dog to go sit in the area with treats, toys, or a comfy cushion for them to sit on. Direct their attention out the window. You can also place them by a window when there is something outside to catch their attention to start this exercise.
3. Observe your dog to see what excites them and to see if anything overwhelms them. Sometimes, watching the mail carrier or chipmunks can be just too much. If this is the case, give your dog a break by closing the curtains or redirecting them to do another activity, and try again at a later time.

4. If your dog continues to show interest in this activity, it can be done for longer periods of time.

How It Helps

Not every enrichment activity has to work your dog physically. By visually taking in the world around them, your dog will be working their brain. Something may catch their attention, or they may relax with the tranquil nature outside. Although you will never know what the day will bring to your dog in this activity, that's what makes it fun and enriching! This activity opens your dog's world to more than just the walls of your home through sights, sounds, and smells.

Observe a Large Crowd

Dogs are sometimes wary or scared of large groups of people. They may be overwhelmed by all the noise, smells, and sights while around a crowd. This activity is perfect for beginning to socialize your puppy or desensitizing your reactive dog. But even the most social dogs may benefit from this activity! You can do this exercise safely by keeping your distance from the crowd and rewarding your pup's calm behaviors. Make sure to give plenty of gentle praise, especially when they lie down and focus on you.

How to Do It

1. Scout out your plan beforehand to make sure you can keep your distance between yourself and a crowd. Some examples include watching a community soccer game at your local field, or going to a park on a weekend day or an outdoor concert going on downtown. You need to make sure that you can stake out a small area where you won't be interrupted by others while training. Sometimes this just entails hanging out with your dog in the trunk of your SUV in a place where there are some familiar smells for your dog to sniff.

2. Set yourself and your dog up in your area. This is a great time to try a training mat, a comfortable blanket, or small rug that can be used in all of your training sessions, no matter the environment. If they have trouble focusing on you in the beginning, ask for a simple behavior, such as sit or lie down.

3. If your dog exhibits calm behaviors, reward with treats, their favorite toy, or verbal praise.

4. If your dog exhibits stress behaviors, such as pacing, pinned ears, or stress yawns, you will need to move farther away from the crowds. Start with a further distance than you think you will need—later on in the session, or a couple sessions later, you may be able to get closer to the crowd without causing stress.
5. Observe the crowds from afar. Your dog may be interested in the crowds, which is great, as long as they are still calm.

Pet Pointers

Wherever you decide to go with your dog, be sure that there is an area where you can hang out undisturbed. In a park, watch the crowd from the top of a small hill; at an outdoor concert space, pick a bench away from the action.

How It Helps

This exercise is absolutely perfect social enrichment for dogs who have a hard time meeting new people, who are working on their calm behaviors, or who just need a switch-up in their everyday routine. It's a flexible activity! By allowing your dog to observe from afar, they can work on their social skills such as being immersed in crowds. However, it's totally fine if your dog remains hesitant with crowds. If observing crowds from a distance is what your dog is comfortable with, allow them that space and choice.

Spend Time with Dog Friends

Whether your dog plays with their puppyhood best friend (your best friend's dog) or goes to a fantastic doggy daycare, the act of socializing with other dogs can be vital to a dog's mental wellness. For some dogs, no matter how long you take them on a walk, it does not get out their energy the same way as running loose around a backyard with a friend. Keep in mind, this enrichment does not apply to reactive dogs (those who bark, leap at, or get overly excited toward other dogs) and dogs who are generally stressed by the presence of other dogs. Only you know how your dog reacts to others. This should be a fun, stress-free activity.

How to Do It

1. If meeting with a friend and their dog, find a place where your dogs can run around after proper introductions, such as a fenced-in yard.

2. If signing your dog up for daycare, be sure to vet the provider by taking a tour of the facility, asking for the staff-to-dog ratio (you want a lower ratio, such as one well-trained staff member to ten dogs) and how big play groups are, seeing where the dogs are put during downtime, and asking for testimonials and reviews.

3. You don't want to completely exhaust your dog with long playtimes. Begin with shorter durations of play (or start with only a few hours at daycare), and you can work your way up to longer stints.

🐾 Pet Pointers 🐾

You can introduce your dogs by going for a short walk around the neighborhood, where they should both show positive body language, such as full-body wagging. If they show negative body language, like whale eyes, stiff movements, or a tucked tail, perhaps your doggy playdate isn't in the cards.

How It Helps

Whether or not dogs are considered pack animals, most do need socialization with other dogs. While you provide all you can for your dog and give them unmatched love, sometimes all your dog may need is some canine affection from their fellow dog. Just like you, sometimes you just want to hang out with your four-legged friend! Daycare or playing with another dog friend is the perfect way to give social enrichment to your dog and physically tire them out without a ton of effort.

Take a Pack Walk

Up the social activity with a pack walk! A pack walk is when one person takes multiple dogs on a walk together. This can be around your neighborhood, or you may have a local business that takes your dog on a longer hike with other dogs. Depending on your dog and the location of the walk, your pup may have to stay on a leash.

How to Do It

1. Take dogs who your dog is friendly with, or if you own multiple dogs, take them all at once (assuming they can walk without tugging or pulling on their leashes).
2. Go on the structured pack walk through your neighborhood or on a hike.
3. Start with a short walk as an introduction, and as your dog seems more comfortable, you can go on longer walks.

Safety Tip

Be sure to use regular leashes during pack walks and leave the retractable leashes at home. The retractable leash is not as reliable and may be easier to knot during a walk if the dogs get excited.

How It Helps

Pack walks are great for socializing dogs in a nonintimidating way because there is no forced interaction and all dogs have a common goal of focusing on the person walking them. This activity also mimics a natural behavior, as wolves often roam in groups. Plus, your dog is tired out and socialized!

Visit with Old Friends

Does your dog have a favorite friend or family member? Invite them over! Dogs have the ability to form strong emotional bonds with humans. While eye contact is seen as hostile in their wolf ancestors, soft eye contact actually helps domestic dogs to bond with the humans in their life. Soft eye contact is when your dog has loose, relaxed body language and may have more dilated pupils. Being around people that your dog enjoys can help them to relieve stress and add some joy into their day.

How to Do It

1. Plan to spend time with a person that your dog likes.
2. Visit a place where your dog is comfortable, such as a park or your friend's home, or have your friend visit your own home.
3. Watch the interactions between your friend and your dog. Make sure your dog is showing relaxation behaviors, such as relaxed body language, no facial tension, and possibly wiggling with happiness.

How It Helps

This kind of social enrichment can help your dog relax because they are in good company. Even just being in the presence of a familiar friend can help to promote calm behaviors. Human bonding was essential in the domestication process of dogs and continues to be beneficial to your furry friend today. This activity also helps your dog build their social skills—especially if they are not used to being around many other people—because your pup can socialize in a way that is familiar and calm.

Meet Other Animals

Lions and tigers and bears, oh my! Well, not quite. Maybe more like macaws and kittens and chinchillas, oh my! Dogs can learn how to play and cohabitate not only with other dogs and humans but also with other animals. It's common to see dogs living with cats, but this can also expand to reptiles, rodents, and birds. You can go even further (if you have the opportunity) by introducing your dog to farm animals as well.

How to Do It

1. Introducing your dog to other animals will (and should!) always take time and will typically take more than one session to be introduced properly. While most times your dog and the other animal will eventually get used to each other, there may be times when your dog can't be around another animal, especially if they don't understand boundaries. Be aware of this and only continue if everyone in the situation is comfortable and safe.

2. If introducing your dog to an animal that lives in your home, let them smell something of the other animal, such as a blanket, so your dog can get the scent of them first.

3. Start slowly after that by allowing your dog to see the other animal from a distance, preferably with a barrier in between (such as a baby gate). If your dog remains calm, take a few steps closer. You should also be watching how the other animal reacts to the situation. If they (or your dog) are showing signs of stress, the activity should end.

4. Work your way up to getting your dog close to the other animal. If it's a farm animal (and your dog is not a trained farm dog), then a barrier should always be in between your dog and the other animal. If the animal is another smaller, household pet, the barrier can be removed if both animals are comfortable.

5. Visits between your dog and another species should always be supervised closely the entire session, and your dog should be removed from the area once the activity is done.

> 🐾 **Pet Pointers** 🐾
>
> When introducing your dog to a cat, make sure the cat has the freedom at all times to get away from your dog, whether it's in a separate room or on a high cat tree. This can give a smoother transition since the cat can move forward on their own time.

How It Helps

Some dogs enjoy the company of others. This activity is a safe way of determining the limits of your pup's social circle. By giving them the opportunity to meet other new animals, you give them an experience that they can't get from other dogs. When meeting new animals, there are new smells and interactions that you can't replicate. This activity can also be important if you have a new animal moving into your home and can help both your dog and the other animal adjust to each other's presence.

Find a Dog-Friendly Coffee Shop

One puppuccino, please. Oh, and a chai latte! Nowadays, there are so many dog-friendly shops, especially if you live in a very dog-friendly city, but smaller towns are starting to come around too. These coffee shops are usually low stress and absolutely *full* of dog lovers. This should be an environment where it's a little safer to have your pup interact with others, but keep an eye on those around you just in case. Find your favorite spot to have a good cup of coffee and hang out with your four-legged best friend.

How to Do It

1. Do your research on what shops and cafés allow dogs. You may have to call around to inquire. Some allow dogs inside, while others may only allow dogs outside on their patio.
2. Bring the necessary items for going out in public. For you, this may mean training treats, a travel water bowl, or maybe a training mat for your dog to lie on. Aim for being overpacked as opposed to unprepared.
3. Visit the coffee shop with your dog.
4. It's up to you how social you want the session to be. While you may have people come up to you and ask to pet your dog, it's perfectly reasonable to say no and that you're working on other skills that don't involve social interaction, such as being calm in public spaces.

Safety Tip 🐾

It's okay to be the voice for your dog. In fact, your dog is count-ing on it! Be polite, but keep your boundaries when it comes to more invasive strangers or children. If they refuse to respect your boundaries, remove yourself and your dog from the situation.

How It Helps

In addition to getting a great cup of cof-fee (or tea), you are helping your dog to learn vital social skills, even if they have zero actual interaction with other humans. Although this activ-ity won't be for every dog, especially reac-tive ones who haven't mastered their social skills yet, it's good practice to show them how to be calm in a  public environment while being stationary and show them that not all strangers are bad. Maybe you'll start with no social interaction and work your way up to making new friends at your local cafe. It's all about progress, not perfection!

NOTES

NOTES

CHAPTER 6

Miscellaneous Enrichment

Sometimes an exercise may have different components, making it hard to be labeled as just one type of enrichment. Or maybe an activity is new and challenging in a way that doesn't fit the mold of any enrichment activity before it! This category of miscellaneous enrichment houses all of those such activities. However, just like the types of enrichment you've seen so far, these enrichment exercises promote natural dog behaviors and can switch up your dog's daily routine.

Play with a Cardboard Food Puzzle

One person's trash is another person's treasure! Or in this case, your dog's treasure. For this activity, save your old cardboard boxes, cardboard paper towel/toilet paper rolls, paper bags, and kraft packing paper, and put them to good use again by making a cardboard food puzzle for your dog. Depending on your dog's needs, you can make it as easy or as challenging as you want.

Cardboard food puzzles are a perfect rainy-day activity that is great for destructive dogs and is an easy DIY project that you can complete in less than ten minutes. The best part is that no two cardboard food puzzles are the same, and you can switch them up each time you make one!

How to Do It

To create a cardboard food puzzle, use your creativity, some of the cardboard boxes and bags lying around, and some treats or kibble. You may manipulate the cardboard however you would like so that it is hiding the food initially from your dog.

1. If you have a puppy or are just starting out in giving your dog enrichment, start out easy by simply putting some kibble in a paper bag, folding over the opening, and giving it to your dog.
2. As your dog starts to understand the activity, make the puzzle more difficult by placing the kibble in a paper bag inside of a cardboard box.
3. If you have an intelligent working breed dog, or your dog is an expert in food puzzles, increase the complexity by adding multiple layers of cardboard and different textures. For example, have a small bag and a bunch of kraft packing

paper in a small box, and put that box in a larger cardboard crate, also filled with newspaper.

4. Cardboard food puzzles should start off easy and get increasingly complex as your dog begins to understand the concept of the game. Starting off with a difficult puzzle can lead to frustration, which is not what we're looking for.

> ### 🐾 Safety Tip 🐾
> Make sure there are no staples, stickers, labels, shipping tape, or bag handles on any materials you give to your dog. These are hazards for your dog and could really hurt them.

How It Helps

This activity is great for enriching a dog's sense of smell and for dogs who love to destroy their toys. It allows them to give in to their natural destructive behaviors without destroying something that you love, such as your couch. By giving them something that you designate they can rip up, you may even find they will stop unwanted chewing elsewhere.

Examine a Phone Book Paper Chain

Looking for a way to recycle those old paper phone books that you have stashed in your basement? Try out this activity for a great way to upcycle! For this exercise, you will need a phone book or printer paper if you don't have a phone book on hand. You will also need a long stick, which you can get from your yard, or you can use a long craft dowel, which can be found at most craft stores.

How to Do It

1. Grab your long stick and begin to take pages from the book, puncturing a hole in the middle of the paper with the stick.
2. Continue to stack the papers on top of each other onto the stick.
3. Crumple the papers up as you go to create a larger volume of space that the paper takes up.
4. Once you add all the paper, go back in and hide treats within the crumpled paper. If you have a small dog, make a short stack of paper. If your dog is large, make the stack taller and more challenging.
5. Give the whole paper-covered stick to your dog and allow them to find all of the treats.

How It Helps

In this activity, your dog uses their nose to find the hidden treats. This will challenge them to work for their food and use their nose and paws to get the goodies.

Chase a Self-Moving Ball

If you want an enrichment activity that you can give to your dog while you're getting a chore done, this one is for you! Just make sure your dog has enough room to run around with their new ball without knocking anything over. Whether you're looking at a vibrating or self-rolling ball, there are many options for you to choose from.

How to Do It

1. Decide which ball you want to use. Some dogs with a prey drive may prefer ones that will roll and that they can chase. Other dogs may prefer a ball that will bounce or vibrate.
2. Supervise your dog during the activity to make sure they do not destroy the ball. Move anything delicate you may be worried about them bumping into.

Safety Tip

Remove the ball once your dog loses interest. All of these toys have batteries in them, which can be potentially harmful if your dog gets to them.

How It Helps

Many dogs have a prey drive, and these toys are skillfully made to mimic prey with their erratic movements. This activity will be very entertaining for your dog and work up their excitement while allowing you to take a break from being your dog's main source of fun.

Hunt for Your Food Game

A discovery game that feeds your pooch their dinner at the same time will become an instant favorite of both yours and your dog's! This is a great rainy-day activity regardless of whether you have a large space available (like a playroom for your pup) or a small space (a 400-foot apartment). Just make sure there aren't any important devices, papers, or other fragile things lying around when you start this game. The main goal of this enrichment exercise is to get your dog to find all the pieces of food you have arranged (not hidden!) throughout your space. The objective is that the food will be placed at different heights and on different surfaces, engaging your pup's brain.

How to Do It

1. Place your dog in a different space or room so they can't see what you're doing. If you are doing this activity for the first time, you may want them to watch you place a few sample pieces of food so that they understand the game.
2. Place, don't hide, treats at different heights and surfaces. Examples include putting one on a chair, on the ground under a table, or on their favorite toy.
3. You don't need to make the activity more challenging by making your dog work to get the treat out of hiding, but you can make it more challenging by using many different heights within the space. This will challenge their body and brain.

4. Let your dog into the space where the food has been carefully placed, and let them use their senses to find the treats around the room.

5. If they need help, show them where one piece of food was placed.

How It Helps

A wolf in the wild would have to use their senses to find food where they could, no matter if it was on the ground or they had to search higher up. Your dog searches just like a wolf does, so this is a great way to see those abilities in action! By moving around the room to work for their food, they will be enriched both physically as well as mentally because they have to use their senses to figure out where all the pieces of food are. No matter how much or how little space you have, you can make this activity exciting and different each time.

Jump Through Hoops

Jumping is a natural behavior for many dogs, and as such, there are many dogs who love to jump! Unfortunately, owners look down on that behavior. Of course, it's rude (and potentially harmful) for a dog to jump on you. So it's perfectly normal to train your dog to use replacement behaviors, such as sitting on a mat or their bed instead of jumping, but your dog may still have the urge to jump. This activity allows them to jump in a safe way that will challenge them mentally and physically. Not all dogs will want to do this activity, but for the very active herding or hunting dogs, this might be just what they need.

How to Do It

1. You can easily find a dog agility hoop online; however, you can also use a Hula-Hoop and manually hold it for this activity. The Hula-Hoop is cheaper and may be something you already have lying around your house. Eventually, you may be able to train your dog to jump through your arms.

2. Train your dog to jump through the hoop. Start with the bottom of the hoop resting on the ground and lure your dog through the hoop. This activity can be done either outside or inside, but if you're just starting out, you will want to begin training outdoors where you can have more room to move around.

3. As your dog gradually begins to understand the exercise, you can raise the hoop. Be aware of your dog's height and figure out a safe distance they can jump up and through the hoop. On average, dogs can typically jump one to three times their height, but that doesn't mean they should do it often. Start with the hoop resting on the ground and work

your way up to no more than two times your dog's height. Puppies and senior dogs should not jump this high and should stick to lower heights to prevent injuring their joints.

> 🐾 **Pet Pointers** 🐾
>
> It's okay if the hoop never makes it more than a few inches off the ground. Not every dog will be keen on jumping heights, or it may be too difficult on their joints. This activity is enriching, no matter the height of the hoop.

How It Helps

With this activity, you may have introduced yourself to a whole new type of training suited for your dog! Hoop jumping is a typical dog agility exercise. Teaching your dog to jump hoops will not only be a great party trick, but it will also physically and mentally challenge your dog. It will also give your dog a safe outlet to perform the jumping behaviors they enjoy without any harm to any humans who may be around.

Transform a Baby Bottle Drying Rack

Some of the best enrichment activities include items not traditionally for dogs. In this activity, you can use an old grass baby bottle drying rack you don't plan to reuse, purchase a new one, or thrift a used one. The "grass" in this drying rack is similar to a combination of a snuffle mat and a food puzzle. It is typically made of thin plastic pieces, which mimic grass and can hold food on the rack. This activity is especially useful for dogs who are not motivated by fabric snuffle mats or dogs who do not rip apart their toys.

How to Do It

1. Once the bottle drying rack is disinfected and ready to go, you can add kibble or treats into the grass.
2. Give the rack to your dog to figure out how to get the treats out of the grass. Monitor them to make sure they are not ripping it apart.

How It Helps

This is a foraging activity for dogs who do not destroy their toys, and it can be helpful during mealtime or on a snack enrichment break. Your dog will have to use their nose to find the food and then find a way to get the food out of the grass.

Make Water Bottle Ice Cubes

The shape of the ice cubes you use in your dog's enrichment can make all the difference! For this activity, purchase thin ice cube trays that are made for fitting properly into plastic water bottles. They are also useful for different enrichment dog toys!

How to Do It

1. After purchasing a thin ice cube tray, fill it with the puréed food or beverage of your choice. For example, bone broth works well for this exercise.
2. Freeze for at least two hours.
3. Place in the enrichment toy of your choosing, such as a Qwizl or a Hol-ee Bone toy. Watch your pup try to get the "ice" cubes out of their toy!

> 🐾 **Switch It Up** 🐾
>
> Besides water, you can use dog-friendly puréed vegetables, broth, or plain Greek yogurt.

How It Helps

These ice cubes make your life easier because they can be prepared beforehand and live in your freezer, allowing you to use them in enrichment as you see fit. Since the treats are frozen, they will enrich your dog's senses and reward them in a different and more challenging way.

Use a Flirt Pole

A flirt pole is essentially a large cat teaser toy. Dogs will enjoy the chasing aspect of the activity, and it will put their brains to the test. The toy is typically a pole with a rope on one end and a toy or ball at the other end of the rope. The flirt pole requires you to participate in the activity and gives you control over how easy or challenging the game will be.

How to Do It

1. While you can easily purchase a flirt pole, you can also make one yourself by checking out many tutorials online. If purchasing, find one that allows you to replace the toy at the end if your dog ends up destroying it.
2. Once you have your flirt pole, entice your dog into doing the activity by showing them the pole and waving it a little to create some motion.

3. Begin to wave the flirt pole around you while your dog chases it. You will want to keep the toy end of the pole close to the ground. If you play higher up, there is a better chance that your dog may hurt themselves. Keeping it on the ground also mimics a prey animal that your dog will want to chase.

4. When your dog catches the toy, let them play with it for a predetermined amount of time, such as a minute or two. This is their reward for catching the "prey." Then repeat the activity as long as your dog shows interest.

> 🐾 **Challenge Accepted** 🐾
>
> This activity is a great time to work on some skills. You can work on their release behavior as well as their "drop it" cue when they catch the toy.

How It Helps

Your dog's preferences may be different than your neighbor's dog, and this includes the way they like to play. This activity is perfect for dogs with a high prey drive, which is a natural instinct for many dogs but may be especially high in hunting or other working dogs. Unless your dog has a specific job to chase after prey, it is ideal that your dog doesn't run after prey animals, which may carry harmful diseases. Thankfully, a flirt pole is a perfect replacement for the prey animals you don't want your dogs to chase.

Use Nail Boards

Nail boards are long pieces of wood, approximately 1—2 feet, that have sandpaper attached to them. These fun boards are very useful as an activity because they take a not fun chore (nail cutting) and turn it into an activity where your pup files down their own nails. This fun object may also be known as a scratch pad. This activity is perfect for pet parents who have difficulty cutting their dog's nails or whose dog won't let them cut their nails. When properly trained, your dog can use the board to allow safe digging behaviors.

How to Do It

1. You can purchase nail boards online, or you can make your own.
2. Begin to train your dog to use the nail board by rewarding any interest in the board, including putting their paws on or near it.
3. Once your dog begins to dig or scratch on the board, you can work up to angling the board up to a 45-degree angle, which will prevent your dog from accidentally scratching up their paw pads.
4. Since this activity will file down your dog's nails, it's important to watch to make sure your dog doesn't overly wear down their nails; however, a majority of dogs will self-regulate and know when to stop. You will want to look for a dog's nail quick, which is pink cuticle that contains a nerve. Everything past that is the nail and can be filed down. The quick can be easily found on a dog with light-colored nails because you can see the clear definition of the pink versus the white or clear nail. On dogs with darker-colored nails, most often you can use a

flashlight shown through the nail to find the quick. Since the quick contains a nerve, your dog will easily be able to feel if they're getting close and will stop.

How It Helps

This exercise is helpful in two ways! It not only helps to keep your dog's nails down to a manageable length; it also mimics digging behaviors. Since many dogs enjoy digging and there are many pet parents who are understandably uncomfortable cutting their dog's nails, this activity is a win-win! Plus, as most dogs are good at self-regulating when their nails get down to a good size, you don't have to guesstimate when to stop cutting their nails.

Grow an Herb Garden

Get out that green thumb—or green paw pad, rather! This enrichment activity is good for your dog and can add a little spice to your meals as an added bonus. This activity is also great because you don't need a yard to grow your herb garden. So, if you happen to live in the city and have a little space near your window, you can still participate. Some easily accessible (and easy-to-grow) herbs that are safe for your dog include basil, dill, mint, and rosemary. For any other herbs you want to grow, do some research and/or contact your vet before planting. Some are definitely not dog friendly!

How to Do It

1. Decide which herbs you want to plant and where you want to plant them. This can be in pots or in your yard. If you decide to use pots, make sure they have drainage holes so the plants can let the water escape as needed. A grow light that you can purchase online may be a great addition if you plant your herbs indoors or during colder months. That way, you can have enrichment fun all year long.

2. After a few weeks of proper care, based on the plant, you should have some herbs sprouting through the soil. If you decide not to grow herbs from seed and prefer to plant seedlings instead, you will be able to utilize the herbs more quickly. Seedling plants can be found at home improvement or local garden stores.

3. Now for the fun part! Let your dog sniff through the herbs once they've grown by giving them access to one potted planter at a time or keeping them tightly leashed in your herb garden.
4. When the herbs are ready to harvest, use them in other enrichment activities, such as sniffing challenges. You can also choose to dry them out (you can find many tutorials online) and save them for a later date.

Pet Pointers

Be careful about planting mint seeds in your yard. Mint can quickly become invasive and take over your garden. This plant is safest in a pot. Other herbs that are best to grow in pots are basil and rosemary, which are great for container gardening.

How It Helps

If you're the kind of pet parent who checks every label of everything that you give to your dog, then you probably know it's difficult to find scents that are not harmful to your dog's sensitive nose. Growing your own herbs is a fun, natural, and safe way to incorporate dog-friendly scents into your dog's enrichment plan. This is a chance to find out your dog's preferences as well. Your dog may prefer one herb over another.

Eat Veggie Kebabs

You may see pet parents do a similar activity with pocket pets (like gerbils, guinea pigs, or hamsters), but veggie kebabs are just as effective for dogs. The basic premise of this exercise is to string some of your dog's favorite vegetables onto cotton twine and hang it so your dog can eat the vegetables off one by one.

How to Do It

1. Cut vegetables into bite-sized pieces. The pieces should be big enough to get a string through but small enough that they will not be choking hazards.
2. Use a plastic yarn sewing needle to thread the string. These kinds of needles can be found at any craft store.
3. Thread the vegetable pieces onto the twine.
4. Remove the plastic needle from the twine.
5. Find a sturdy place that your dog can reach to hang your veggie kebab from, such as a deck railing.
6. Let your dog engage with the veggie kebab.
7. Once your dog finishes all of the vegetables on the string, remove the twine from your dog's reach.

How It Helps

The veggie kebab activity is a great way to introduce vegetables into your dog's life while making it fun. Dogs typically eat most, if not all, of their food off of the ground. By raising the food up and making them work for it, you create an enticing activity that they don't run into every day.

Use Chew Toys

Purchase your dog's toys in a way that will optimize their enrichment plan (as well as their happiness)! Make sure your fur baby has a number of different types of toys. Having access to chew toys for your dog is a great way to prevent destruction of household items and stifle boredom. Chew toys can include anything from puppy teething toys to rubber or natural bones to safe rope toys.

How to Do It

1. Decide on which toys you feel comfortable giving to your dog. Ask a veterinarian or look on factual websites for guidance.
2. Test out which ones your dog enjoys playing with.
3. Take note of your dog's favorites and add them to your rotation of toys.
4. To prevent dental damage, remove the chew toy after about an hour if your dog is constantly chewing.

How It Helps

Chewing is a behavior that is completely natural and normal for dogs! Because you can't train it out of your dogs, giving them the proper and safe chew toys to gnaw on will allow them to exhibit their natural behavior while also preventing undesired destruction in your house. When you also keep your dog's favorite chew toys on rotation, you can keep them excited about their "new" toy each week.

Play with a Papier-Mâché Ball

Let's bring back some childhood arts and crafts! Though your dog can't really participate in the construction of this fun toy, they will certainly appreciate your hard work in putting this together for them. Reminder: Though it's fun to decorate, painting this ball is likely not pet friendly. For this activity, you will make your papier-mâché out of paper, flour, water, and cinnamon and construct it to make a feeder toy for your dog. Since the materials are all dog friendly, your dog can destroy the papier-mâché as well.

How to Do It

1. To construct the ball: Add half a cup of flour to half a cup of water.
2. Add in a dash of cinnamon to your flour and water mixture. Mix it all up together. The cinnamon gives the ball a fun scent that your dog will love!
3. Blow a balloon up to the desired size of your ball. Consider your dog's size. Tie a knot to secure the size and put it to the side.
4. Tear newspaper or printer paper into strips. If you use newspaper, make sure there are no staples.
5. Dip the newspaper strips into your flour mixture one by one.
6. Place the dipped newspaper strips onto the balloon, leaving a small hole at the top where you can add in food or treats. Make sure the hole isn't so small that your dog can get their head stuck.
7. Let the balloon sit until it is dried. This may take a few hours.
8. Once dry, pop the balloon. It should remove easily. Make sure there are no remaining rubber parts of the balloon, as they may be a choking hazard for your dog.

9. Add food or treats to the papier-mâché feeder and let your dog destroy it. Keep close supervision, as it's best not to let your dog consume the paper itself.

> ### 🐾 Switch It Up 🐾
> Experiment with trying other scents while making the papier-mâché. Try adding some ginger, dill herb, or dried rosemary to give your project a strong, dog-friendly smell that will entice your dog. Before mixing in any scent, make sure your dog likes it.

How It Helps

Creating a papier-mâché feeder toy for your dog is not only a way to recycle old newspapers you no longer need, but it also gets you involved in a creative process to help enrich your dog! What a great recycling project. If your dog is prone to destroying their toys, this activity can help encourage their destructive behaviors in a safe way that gives them the satisfaction they are looking for.

Paint with Your Dog

Help your dog become an artist! This activity can be fun for you and your dog, giving you a keepsake that you can cherish forever. This exercise requires kid-safe paint, a flat canvas board, newspaper, and high-value treats for your dog. A kiddie pool is optional for a fast cleanup. The best place to paint with your dog is outside, preferably on the grass, to prevent a mess indoors. Not only will this activity get your dog up and moving around; it will also give them some time to bond with you. Remember to let your pup's artistic vision shine—while it's okay to guide them to step in certain ways, understand that you may not get a perfect set of paw prints.

How to Do It

1. Place newspaper on the floor or the ground outside, or if you are using a kiddie pool, place the newspaper down on the bottom of the kiddie pool.
2. Place your canvas in the center of the newspaper.
3. Decide which paint colors you want to use. The best way to ensure your dog will step on the paint is to squirt the paint out of the bottle like you normally would, then use your fingers to spread the paint around the canvas. Don't thin the paint too much around the canvas, or the paint will dry before your dog can walk through.

4. Lure your dog to walk through the paint and onto the canvas using their treats. Watch the comfort level of your dog. If they do not want to do the activity, their body language will let you know.

5. Once the activity is complete, wash your dog's paws to get any remaining paint off of their pads and fur. This can be done simply with water and a washcloth, but if you find the paint is stubborn in coming off of your dog's paws, use dog-friendly soap.

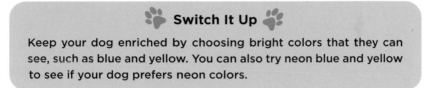

Switch It Up

Keep your dog enriched by choosing bright colors that they can see, such as blue and yellow. You can also try neon blue and yellow to see if your dog prefers neon colors.

How It Helps

Painting with your dog is not an activity you get to do every day. Doing an activity like this will help them switch up their routine and give them a different sensation of walking through paint. When you're done with the painting, sign your dog's name and date on the back of the canvas. Repeat this activity enough, and you'll be able to start your own doggy art gallery!

Play with Burrow Toys

Balls, rope toys, chew toys, feeders—there are so many types of toys! This activity is modeled after a burrow toy. The concept of a burrow toy is pretty straightforward: You have one hollow plush toy with multiple openings that are filled with smaller, squeaky plush toys. The goal for the dog is to remove the smaller toys from the larger toy.

Burrow toys are the perfect quiet-time activity for your dog and are especially great for dogs who love to destroy their toys or who love a good puzzle challenge. These toys are easy to find online or in most home goods and pet stores, and they come in many shapes and forms to keep your pup interested and excited.

How to Do It

1. Find a burrow toy that is an appropriate size for your dog. If you have a larger breed, don't choose a burrow toy for a small dog.
2. Stuff the smaller toys into the larger hollow toy.
3. Let your dog go nuts! Your dog will have to work to get each small squeaky plush out of the larger toy. They can use their teeth, nails, or nose—whatever gets the job done.

4. Once they get the smaller toys out, just stuff them back into the bigger plush to restart the game.

5. These small plush toys may not last very long if your dog is a heavy chewer. Toys, especially plush toys, have a limited life span but can add a whole lot of joy to your dog's everyday routine.

> ## 🐾 Safety Tip 🐾
>
> If your dog has a history of ingesting the stuffing from inside a toy, you will want to closely monitor their playtime with burrow toys.

How It Helps

Burrow toys fulfill an instinctual need for dogs: the natural desire to rip and tear apart their prey, also known as their prey drive. A dog's prey drive is the instinctive inclination to hunt and capture a prey animal. Most dogs have this drive, but it is especially prevalent in working breed dogs, such as Boxers, Saint Bernards, Samoyeds, and more. It's incredibly difficult, if not impossible, to fully train the prey drive out of your dog. It's just not natural for them to ignore their drive! So instead, learn how to embrace it. Additionally, if you are experiencing destruction of furniture, shoes, or anything else, it is worth giving burrow toys a try. Redirecting your pup's behavior so they focus on the burrow toy teaches your dog what are chewable toys versus what is off-limits.

Enjoy an Outdoor Solar Fountain

Picture this: It's a warm, sunny summer day in your yard. Your dog can just lie down and relax, watching the leaves blow and the birds chirp. Sounds relaxing, right? Now add in an outdoor fountain for some relaxing sounds. It's like a meditation day for your dog!

How to Do It

1. Purchase a solar outdoor fountain that you can place anywhere in your backyard. There are also solar bird baths that can attach to a rail.
2. Let your dog bask in the sunlight while the fountain does its job.

How It Helps

This activity can fit in multiple categories. It is sensory enrichment because of the sounds of the fountain. It is environmental enrichment because it is something added into your dog's environment that is not normally there. It can be social enrichment if birds or other animals decide to visit the fountain. If it's clean enough (no other animals have used the fountain), your dog may even decide to drink from the fountain, making it food enrichment. Something so simple in your environment can make a huge difference in your dog's life.

NOTES

NOTES

Resources
Guide

Bindi's Bucket List
www.bindisbucketlist.com

Effects of Environmental Enrichment on Dog Behaviour: Pilot Study
www.ncbi.nlm.nih.gov/pmc/articles/PMC8772568/

The Ohio State University Indoor Pet Initiative: Environmental Enrichment
https://indoorpet.osu.edu/dogs/
environmental_enrichment_dogs

Outward Hound Furtropolis
www.outwardhound.com/furtropolis/

Positively: Dog Enrichment
https://positively.com/dog-wellness/dog-enrichment/

Purdue University Canine Welfare Science: Environmental Enrichment
https://caninewelfare.centers.purdue.edu/behavior/
enrichment/

Tufts University Center for Shelter Dogs Resource Library
https://centerforshelterdogs.tufts.edu/resource-library/

Books

Adventure Dogs: Activities to Share with Your Dog—From Comfy Couches to Mountain Tops **by Fern Watt**

The Big Book of Tricks for the Best Dog Ever: A Step-by-Step Guide to 118 Amazing Tricks and Stunts **by Larry Kay and Chris Perondi**

Canine Body Language: A Photographic Guide Interpreting the Native Language of the Domestic Dog **by Brenda Aloff**

Canine Confidential: Why Dogs Do What They Do **by Marc Bekoff**

The Dog Behavior Answer Book, 2nd Edition: Understanding and Communicating with Your Dog and Building a Strong and Happy Relationship **by Arden Moore**

How Dogs Work: A Head-to-Tail Guide to Your Canine **by Daniel Tatarsky and David Humphries**

Organizations

American Kennel Club: Expert Advice
www.akc.org/expert-advice/

ASPCApro: Canine Enrichment
www.aspcapro.org/enrichment-behavior/canine-enrichment

Companion Animal Psychology: All about Dogs
www.companionanimalpsychology.com/p/all-about-dogs.html

Dogs Playing for Life
https://dogsplayingforlife.com

Social Media

Beyond the Bowl—Canine Enrichment Facebook Group
www.facebook.com/groups/1747279312231501

Canine Enrichment Ideas Facebook Group
www.facebook.com/groups/2326424080971527

DIY Canine Enrichment Toys
www.facebook.com/groups/DIYCanineEnrichment

Index

About the Author

Chelsea Barstow holds a bachelor of science degree in zoology from the University of New Hampshire and is a certified canine enrichment technician (DN-CET). As a former zookeeper, she has spent many years in hands-on practice becoming an expert in animal enrichment. She now shares her passion and learning through her social media presence, @chelsbars, accumulating a rapidly growing community of tens of thousands of appreciative pet parents. Chelsea lives in Connecticut with her husband and two dogs. She spends her free time trying to find the best iced coffee in the state.